Contemporary Social Mobility
&
Social Movements

Contemporary Social Mobility
&
Social Movements

Views and Reviews

S.C. Joshi

FORWARD BOOKS
New Delhi • Guwahati • Visakhapatnam

FORWARD BOOKS
4649-B/21, Ansari Road
Darya Ganj, New Delhi - 110 002
Ph.: 23263193 / 9811582579 / 09435116718
Fax: 011-23263193
Email: ektabooks@yahoo.com
www.akanshapublishinghouse.com

Contemporary Social Mobility and Social Movements

First Published 2011

Reprint Edition, 2026

ISBN 978-81-909742-8-8

PRINTED IN INDIA

Published by Forward Books, New Delhi and Printed at Harmain Offset Press, Delhi.

Contents

Preface

Every society in the world faces the challenge of social inequality and deprivation. Certain sections of society are discriminated on the pretext of race, colour, gender, caste and socioeconomic considerations all over the world. Weaker sections and women have been more vulnerable to these social evils. In caste-ridden societies like India these problems are more acute. The down-trodden low caste people suffered/ being suffering the pangs of untouchability and low socioeconomic status. They were maltreated and discriminated in all walks of life and so called upper castes perpetrated heinous crimes against them.

Though it's the prime duty of state to ensure equality of opportunities and basic human rights of all its subjects, yet the condition of marginalized and excluded sections could not be ameliorated. Many social upheavals occurred and social movements were launched by social reformers during different time phases. As such social mobility and social movements have attracted the attention of intelligentsia.

Here in the present volume we have tried to portray a picture of social mobility and social movements from sociological perspective. All pertinent issues are suitably addressed with examples and experiences. The following chapters make core of the study—Civil Society and Relevant Issues; Social Movement: Genesis and Salient Features; Social Movements in India; Role of Social Change; Social

Action and Social Control; Reconceptualising Social Movement; Notable Social Movements; Social Reform Movements; Dalit Movement in India: An Overview; Social Mobility and Public Opinion; Appendix and Bibliography etc.

Hopefully, students, researchers and teachers of sociology, political science and economics will find this of utmost use.

Our description is substantially based on the write-ups of various scholars of repute in this field. We are deeply beholden to them all. We express gratitude to the sources of information too. My seniors, colleagues and friends rendered all assistance and support while working on this. I am grateful to them all. Finally I am thankful to my publishers for undertaking publication of this work.

—SCJ

1

Civil Society and Relevant Issues

First it is pertinent to note that the term civil society was used by writers such as Locke and J.J. Rousseau to describe civil government as differentiated from natural society or the state of nature. The Marxist concept derives from Hegel. In Hegel civil or bourgeois society as the realm of individuals who have left the unity of the family to enter into economic competition is contrasted with the state or political society.

Marx uses the concept of civil society in his critique of Hegel. It is used as a yardstick of the change from feudal to bourgeoisie society. Civil society arose, Marx insists from the destruction of medieval society. Previously individuals were part of many different societies such as guilds or estates each of which had a political role so that there was no separate civil realm.

As these partial societies broke down, civil society arose in which the individual became all important. The old bonds of privilege were replaced by the selfish needs of atomistic individuals separated from each other and from the community.

It is apt to mention that the fragmented conflictual nature of civil society with its property relations necessitates a type of politics which does not reflect this conflict but is abstracted and removed from it. The modern state is made necessary and at the same time limited by the characteristics of civil society. The fragmentation and misery of civil society escape the control of the state which is limited to formal negative activities and is rendered impotent by the conflict which is the essence of economic life.

The political identity of individuals as citizens in modern society is severed from their civil identity and from their function in the productive sphere as tradesmen, day labor or landowner. Although Gramsci continues to use the term to refer to the private or non state sphere, including the economy, his picture of civil society is very different from that of Marx.

Gramsci insists on its complex organization as the ensemble of organisms commonly called private where hegemony and spontaneous consent are organized. He argues that any distinction between civil society and the state is only methodological since even a policy of non intervention like laissez faire is established by the state itself. A fully developed civil society is presented as a trench system able to resist the incursions of economic crises and to protect the state.

Whereas Marx insists on the separation between the state and civil society, Gramsci emphasizes the inter relationship between the two. The state narrowly conceived as government is protected by hegemony organized in civil society while the coercive state apparatus fortifies the hegemony of the dominant class.

In any actual society the lines of democration between civil society and the state may be blurred but Gramsci argues against any attempt to equate or identify the two.

And while he accepts a role for the state in developing civil society, he warns against perpetuating state worship.

Gramsci redefines the withering away of the state in terms of a full development of the self-regulating attributes of civil society. In fact, in 'Marx's writings civil society is portrayed as the terrain of individual egotism.

Civil Society and Social Movement

It must be remembered that social movements and civil society have structures like organizations a well identified leadership and ideology. Civil society initiatives and social movements are social processes which undergo several stages of progression from mobilization to intensive collective action. Social movements and civil societies pledge for change in the established order of society.

However some of them also work to resist change in society. They both occupy civil space in society. The creation of new collective identity is an essential part of both social movements and civil society. They are based on identified ideological choices. They are initiated by enterprising people for the maximization of specific interests. Here both processes can be taken over by the state.

Social movements are broader categories or agencies. At times it even looks for radical change by attacking the existing structure of the society. Civil society looks for gradual change within the existing arrangement. Civil society at times asks political questions and political solutions through developmental activities.

Civil Society and Marginalization

In fact, marginalization has been defined as a complex process of relegating specific groups of people to the lower or outer edge of society. It effectively pushes these groups of people to the margin of society economically, politically, culturally and socially following the policy of exclusion.

It denies a section of the society equal access to productive resources and avenues for the realization of their productive human potential and opportunities for their full capacity utilization. This pushes the community to poverty, misery, low wage and discrimination and livelihood insecurity. Their upward social mobility is being limited.

Politically this process of relegation denies people equal access to the formal power structure and participation in the decision making processes leading to their subordination to and dependence on the economically and politically dominant groups of society. As a consequence of the economic, political and cultural deprivation a vast chunk of the population has emerged to be socially ignorant, illiterate, uneducated and dependent.

Devoid of the basic necessities of life they are relegated to live on the margins of society. In developing countries like India, civil societies have assumed much significant role for the social development of the marginalized people. The marginalized community look upon the civil society with expectation as state's development initiatives have failed to percolate to the bottom strata of the society.

In the contemporary development scenario, the concept of empowerment of the marginalized has got a special focus and civil society initiatives have been given special emphasis. As the role of civil society has acquired a role for the social development, it has developed relationship with marginalized community.

It must be remembered that the development process

has failed to end the deprivation faced by the marginalized communities in most of the developing nations.Infact it has contributed to the social reproduction of marginalization.

According to Human Development Report the marginalized people are emerged as victims of these processes of development. In every society there are some sections of people who are deprived of socio-economic opportunities for their sustenance and are victims of social, cultural and political exclusion. In India the marginalized communities are rural poor, scheduled tribes and castes, manual workers in unorganized sectors etc.The marginalized people have very little or no participation in the development process.

The initiatives are channeled through pre-existing power structure. Their conditions have remained unchanged over the centuries even after government initiatives implemented for their upward mobility. There has been serious thinking about the participation of marginalized communities in the process of development.

Due to government failure of integrating them in the development process, an alternative has emerged in the form of civil society to evolve the strategy for empowerment of the marginalized people.

In a welfare state under civil society, it is the prime duty of state to empower the marginalized sections of society. Empowerment is a political process. The core idea of empowerment lies in the dynamics of sharing, distribution and redistribution of power.

According to Max Weber, power is one's capacity to have control over others and when this capacity to control is legitimized, it becomes authority. The logic of empowerment essentially involves the dynamics of authority. Powerlessness has been legitimized within the given social order.

Hence empowerment will mean a process of distribution of power through legitimized means. In human society everybody has no equal authority as people have unequal access to the resources that determine power.

Remarkably, the process of gaining control over self, ideology, material and knowledge resources which determine power may be termed empowerment. Thus the process of gaining control over resources is to be seen within the given context of deprivation, structure of hierarchy and the process of legitimization and reproduction. The civil societies try to ensure the equal access to the resources to the marginalized community that determines power equation with in the society.

After having a look at the cause of marginalized people in a civil society, now let us focus on social inequality and exclusion, which have led to social mobilization. In customary developing countries like India many social movement centres around social inequality and exclusion.

SOCIAL INEQUALITY AND EXCLUSION

It is pertinent to note that in every society some people have a greater share of valued resources e.g. money, property, education, health and power than others. These social resources can be divided into three forms of capital—economic capital in the form of material assets and income; cultural capital such as educational qualifications and status; and social capital in the form of networks of contacts and social associations. Often these three forms of capital overlap and one can be converted into the other. For example a person from a well-off family can afford expensive higher education and so can acquire cultural or educational capital.

Patterns of unequal access to social resources are

commonly called social inequality. Social inequality reflects innate differences between individuals for example their varying abilities and efforts. Someone may be endowed with exceptional intelligence or talent or may have worked very hard to achieve their wealth and status.

However by and large social inequality is not the outcome of innate or natural differences between people but is produced by the society in which they live.

Prejudices

Prejudices refer to pre-conceived opinions or attitudes held by members of one group towards another. The word literally means pre-judgement that is an opinion formed in advance of any familiarity with the subject before considering any available evidence.

A prejudiced person's preconceived views are often based on hearsay rather than on direct evidence and are resistant to change even in the face of new information. Prejudice may be either positive or negative. Although the word is generally used for negative pre-judgements, it can also apply to favourable pre-judgement. For example a person may be prejudiced in favour of members of his/her own caste or group and without any evidence –believe them to be superior to members of other castes or groups.

Stereotypes

It must be remembered that rejudices are often grounded in stereotypes, fixed and inflexible characterisations of a group of people. Stereotypes are often applied to ethnic and racial groups and to women. In a country such as India which was colonised for a long time many of these stereotypes are partly colonial creations.

Some communities were characterised as martial races

some others as effeminate or cowardly yet others as untrustworthy. In both English and Indian fictional writings we often encounter an entire group of people classified as lazy or cunning. It may indeed be true that some individuals are sometimes lazy or cunning, brave or cowardly. But such a general statement is true of individuals in every group. Stereotypes fix whole groups into single, homogenous categories; they refuse to recognise the variation across individuals and across contexts or across time. They treat an entire community as though it were a single person with a single all-encompassing trait or characteristic.

Discrimination

Simultaneously, if prejudice describes attitudes and opinions, discrimination refers to actual behaviour towards another group or individual. Discrimination can be seen in practices that disqualify members of one group from opportunities open to others as when a person is refused a job because of their gender or religion. Discrimination can be very hard to prove because it may not be open or explicitly stated. Discriminatory behaviour or practices may be presented as motivated by other more justifiable, reasons rather than prejudice. For example the person who is refused a job because of their caste may be told that they were less qualified than others and that the selection was done purely on merit.

State and Non-State Initiatives

It is apt to mention that the Indian state has had special programmes for the Scheduled Tribes and Scheduled Castes since even before Independence. The Schedules listing the castes and tribes recognized as deserving of special treatment because of the massive discrimination practiced against them were drawn up in 1935 by the British Indian Government.

After Independence the same policies have been continued and many new ones added. Amongst the most significant additions is the extension of special programmes to the Other Backward Classes since the early 1990s.The most important state initiative attempting to compensate for past and present caste discrimination is the one popularly known as reservations. This involves the setting aside of some places or seats for members of the Scheduled Castes and Tribes in different spheres of public life. These include reservation of seats in the State and Central legislatures; reservation of jobs in government service across all departs and public sector companies and reservation of seats in educational institutions.

The proportion of reserved seats is equal to the percentage share of the SC and STs in the total population. But for the OBCs this proportion is decided differently. The same principle is extended to other developmental programmes of the government, some of which are exclusively for the SC or ST while others give them preference.

Besides the reservations there have been a number of laws passed to end, prohibit and punish caste discrimination; especially untouchability.One of the earliest such laws was the Caste Disabilities Removal Act of 1850 which disallowed the curtailment of rights of citizens due solely to change of religion or caste. The most recent such law was the Constitution Amendment Act of 2005 which became law on 23rd January 2006. Coincidentally both the 1850 law and the 2006 amendment related to Backward Classes in institutions of higher education while the 1850 Act was used to allow entry of dalits to government schools.

In between there have been numerous laws of which the important ones are the Constitution of India itself, passed in 1950 and the Scheduled Castes and Scheduled Tribes Prevention of Atrocities Act of 1989.

It is significant to note that the Constitution abolished untouchability and introduced the reservation provisions. The 1989 Prevention of Atrocities Act revised and strengthened the legal provisions punishing acts of violence or humiliation against Dalits and adivasis.The fact that legislation was passed repeatedly on this subject is proof of the fact that the law alone cannot end a social practice. State action alone cannot ensure social change.

No social group however weak or oppressed is only a victim. Human beings are always capable of organizing and acting on their own –often against very heavy odds to struggle for justice and dignity. Dalits too have been increasingly active on the political, agitational and cultural fronts. Recently Dalits have become aggessive and a process of polarisation is in continuance.

From the pre-Independence struggles and movements launched by people like Jyotiba Phule, Periyar, Ambedkar and others to contemporary political organizations like the Bahujan Samaj Party in Uttar Pradesh or the Dalit Sangharsh Samiti of Karnataka, Dalit political assertion has come a long way. Dalits have also made significant contributions to literature in several Indian languages specially Marathai, Kannada, Tamil, Telugu and Hindi. Many Institutions and centres are active to study the cause of dalits in India.

The Other Backward Classes

In fact, untouchability was the most visible and comprehensive form of social discrimination. However there were a large group of castes that were of low status and were also subjected to varying levels of discrimination short of untouchability.These were the service and artisanal castes who occupied the lower rungs of the caste hierarchy. The Constitution of India recognises the possibility that there may be groups other than the SC and STs who suffer from social disadvantages and marginalisation.

These groups which need not be based on caste alone but generally are identified by caste were described as the socially and educationally backward classes. This is the constitutional basis of the popular term Other Backward Classes. The OBCs are defined negatively by what they are not. They are neither part of the forward castes at the upper end of the status spectrum nor of the dalits at the lower end. But since caste has entered all the major Indian religions and is not confined to Hinduism alone, there are also members of other religions who belong to the backward castes and share the same traditional occupational identification and similar or worse socio-economic status.

Since the 1990s there has been resurgence of lower caste movements in north India among both the Dalits and OBCs.The politicisation of the OBCs allows them to convert their large numbers recent surveys show that they are about 41% of the national population into political influence. This was not possible at the national level before as shown by the sidelining of the Kalelkar Commission report and the neglect of the Mandal Commission report.

The large disparities between the upper OBCs and the lower OBCs make this a difficult political category to work with. However the OBCs are severely under represented in all spheres except landholding and political representation. Although the upper OBCs are dominant in the rural sector the situation of urban OBCs is much worse being much closer to that of the SC and STs than to the upper castes.

Tribal and Social Inequality

The STs are social groups recognized by the Indian Constitution as specially marked by poverty, powerlessness and social stigma. The jana or tribes were believed to be people of the forest whose distinctive habitat in the hill and forest areas shaped their economic, social and political attributes. Tribal groups have had long and close association with Hindu society and culture making the boundaries between tribe and caste quite porous.

Apparently, the Independence of India in 1947 should have made life easier for adivasis but this is not the case. Firstly the govt monopoly over forests continued leading to acceleration in exploitation of forests. Secondly the policy of capital intensive industrialization adopted by the Indian govt required mineral resources and power generation capacities which were concentrated in Adivasi lands.

Adivasi lands were rapidly acquired for new mining and dam projects. In the process millions of Adivasis were displaced without any appropriate compensation or rehabilitation. Justified in the name of national development and economic growth these policies were also a form of internal colonialism, subjugating adivasis and alienating the resources upon which they depended. Projects such as Sardar Sarovar Dam on the river Narmada in western India and the Polavaram dam on the river Godavari in AP will displace hundred and thousands of adivasis driving them to greater destitution. These processes continue to prevail and have become even more powerful since the 1990s when economic liberalization policies were officially adopted by the government of India.

It is pertinent to note that the term Adivasi connotes political awareness and the assertion of rights. Literally meaning original inhabitants the term was coined in the 1930s as part of the struggle against the intrusion by the colonial govt and outside settlers and moneylenders. Being adivasi is about shared experiences of the loss of forests, the alienation of land, repeated displacements since Independence in the name of development projects and much more.

Remarkably, in spite of the heavy odds against them and in the face of their marginalization many tribal groups have been wagging struggles against outsiders and the state. In post-Independence India, the most significant achievements of Adivasi movements include the attainment of statehood for Jharkhand and Chattisgarh which were originally part of Bihar and Madhya Pradesh respectively.

Disabled and Social Inequality

Physical and mental retardation are genetic and biological problems as many people are challenged by these irrespective of caste, religion or race. The differently abled are not disabled only because they are physically or mentally impaired but also because society is built in a manner that does not cater to their needs. In contrast to the struggles over Dalit, adivasi or women's rights the rights of the disabled have been recognized only very recently. Yet in all historical periods, in all societies there have been people who are disabled.

It must be remembvered that in India labels such as disability, handicap, crippled, blind and deaf are used synonymously. Often these terms are hurled at people as insults. In culture that looks up to bodily perfection all deviations from the perfect body signify abnormality, defect and distortion. Labels such as bechara accentuate the victim status for the disabled person. The roots of such attitudes lie in the cultural conception that views an impaired body as a result of fate.

Destiny is seen as the culprit and disabled people are the victims. The common perception views disability as retribution for past karma from which there can be no reprieve. The dominant cultural construction in India therefore looks at disability as essentially a characteristic of the individual. The popular images in mythology portray the disabled in an extremely negative fashion.

It is pertinent to note that the term disabled challenges each of these assumptions. Terms such as mentally challenged, visually impaired and physically impaired came to replace the more negative terms such as retarded, crippled or lame. The disabled are rendered disabled not because they are biologically disabled but because society renders them so. The social construction of disability has yet another dimension.

There is a close relationship between disability and poverty.Malnutrition, mothers weakened by frequent childbirth, inadequate immunization programmes, and accidents in overcrowded homes all contribute to an incidence of disability among poor people that is higher than among people living in easier circumstances. Furthermore disability creates and exacerbates poverty by increasing isolation and economic strain not just for the individual but for the family there is little doubt that disabled people are among the poorest in poor countries.

It is only recently with the efforts of the disabled themselves that some awareness is building in society on the need to rethink disability.

Recognition of disability is absent from the wider

educational discourse. This is evident from the historical practices within the educational system that continue to marginalize the issue of disability by maintaining two separate streams—one for disabled students and one for everyone else i.e. general class.

Gender Issue

It is apt to mention here that because of the obvious biological and physical differences between men and women, gender inequality is often treated as natural. However despite appearances, scholars have shown that the inequalities between men and women are social rather than natural. There are no biological reasons that can explain why so few women are found in position of public power. Nor can nature explain why women generally receive a smaller or no share in family property in most societies. But the strongest argument comes from the societies that were different from the normal or common pattern.

If women were biologically unfit to be inheritors and head of families how did matrilineal societies work for centuries? How have women managed to be successful farmers and traders in so many African societies? There is nothing biological about the inequalities that mark the relations between men and women. Gender is thus also a form of social inequality and exclusion like caste and class but with its own specific features.

Though gender equality is currently a declared policy of state and statutory provision have been there to check gender discrimination, the condition of women in all societies in general and in developing countries like India in particular is still pitiable. And female sex is discriminated in all aspects.

2

Social Movement: Genesis and Salient Features

In common parlance, by social movements we mean a type of group action. They are large informal groupings of individuals and/or organizations focused on specific political or social issues, in other words, on carrying out, resisting or undoing a social change.

Remarkably, Charles Tilly defines social movements as a series of contentious performances, displays and campaigns by which ordinary people made collective claims on others. For Tilly, social movements are a major vehicle for ordinary people's participation in public politics. He argues that there are three major elements to a social movement:

1. ***Campaigns:*** a sustained, organized public effort making collective claims of target authorities;
2. ***Repertoire (repertoire of contention)***: employment of combinations from among the following forms of political action: creation of special-purpose associations and coalitions, public meetings, solemn processions, vigils, rallies, demonstrations, petition drives, statements to and in public media, and pamphleteering; and
3. ***WUNC displays:*** participants' concerted public

> representation of worthiness, unity, numbers, and commitments on the part of themselves and/or their constituencies.

Further Sidney Tarrow defines a social movement as collective challenges [to elites, authorities, other groups or cultural codes] by people with common purposes and solidarity in sustained interactions with elites, opponents and authorities. He specifically distinguishes social movements from political parties and advocacy groups.

It is apt to mention that modern Western social movements became possible through education (the wider dissemination of literature), and increased mobility of labor due to the industrialization and urbanization of 19th century societies. It is sometimes argued that the freedom of expression, education and relative economic independence prevalent in the modern Western culture is responsible for the unprecedented number and scope of various contemporary social movements. However others point out that many of the social movements of the last hundred years grew up, like the Mau Mau in Kenya, to oppose Western colonialism. Either way, social movements have been and continued to be closely connected with democratic political systems.

Occasionally social movements have been involved in democratizing nations, but more often they have flourished after democratization. Over the past 200 years, they have become part of a popular and global expression of dissent.

Modern movements often utilize technology and the internet to mobilize people globally. Adapting to communication trends is a common theme among successful movements.

Political science and sociology have developed a variety of theories and empirical research on social movements.

For example, some research in political science highlights the relation between popular movements and the formation of new political parties as well as discussing the function of social movements in relation to agenda setting and influence on politics.

It is apt to mention that the term "social movements" was introduced in 1850 by the German Sociologist Lorenz von Stein in his book *"History of the French Social Movement from 1789 to the Present"* (1850).

Tilly argues that the early growth of social movements was connected to broad economic and political changes including parliamentarization, market capitalization, and proletarianization. Political movements that evolved in late 18th century, like those connected to the French Revolution and the Polish Constitution of May 3, 1791 are among the first documented social movements, although Tilly notes that the British abolitionist movement has "some claim" to be the first social movement (becoming one between the sugar boycott of 1791 and the second great petition drive of 1806).

The labor movement and socialist movement of the late 19th century are seen as the prototypical social movements, leading to the formation of communist and social democratic parties and organisations. From 1815, Britain after victory in the Napoleonic Wars entered a period of social upheaval. Similar tendencies were seen in other countries as pressure for reform continued, for example in Russia with the Russian Revolution of 1905 and of 1917, resulting in the collapse of the Russian State around the end of the World War I.

In 1945, Britain after victory in the World War II entered a period of radical reform and change. In the post-war period, women's rights, gay rights, peace, civil rights, anti-nuclear and environmental movements emerged, often dubbed the *New Social Movements*. They led, among other things, to the formation of green parties and organisations influenced by the new left. Some find in the end of the 1990s the emergence of a new global social movement, the anti globalization movement. Some social movement scholars posit that with the rapid pace of globalization, the potential for the emergence of new *type* of social movement is latent—they make the analogy to national movements of the past to describe what has been termed a global citizens movement.

Key Processes

- Urbanization led to larger settlements, where people of similar goals could find each other, gather and organize. This facilitated social interaction between scores of people, and it was in urban areas that those early social movements first appeared.
- Similarly, the process of industrialization which gathered large masses of workers in the same region explains why many of those early social movements addressed matters such as economic wellbeing, important to the worker class.
- Many other social movements were created at universities, where the process of mass education brought many people together.
- With the development of communication technologies, creation and activities of social movements became easier
- From printed pamphlets circulating in the 18th century coffeehouses to newspapers and Internet, all those tools became important factors in the growth of the social movements. Finally, the spread of democracy and political rights like the freedom of speech made the creation and functioning of social movements much easier.

Types of Social Movement

Sociologists distinguish between several types of social movement:

1. *By Scope*
   (a) *radical movement* -movements dedicated to changing value systems in a fundamental way. Examples would include the American Civil Rights Movement which demanded full civil rights and equality under the law to all Americans, regardless of race; the Polish Solidarity (*Solidarnoœæ*) movement which demanded the transformation of a Stalinist political and economic system into a democracy; or the South African shack dwellers' movement Abahlali baseMjondolo which demands the full inclusion of shack dwellers into the life of cities.
   (b) *reform movement* -movements advocating changing some norms or laws. Examples of such a movement would include a trade union with a goal of increasing workers rights, a green movement advocating a set of ecological laws, or a movement supporting introduction of a capital punishment or the right to abortion. Some reform movements may aim for a change in custom and moral norms, such as condemnation of pornography or proliferation of some religion.
2. *By Type of Change*
   (a) conservative movement movements which want to preserve existing norms, values, etc. For example, the anti-technology 19th century Luddites movement or the modern movement

opposing the spread of the genetically modified food could be seen as conservative movements in that they aimed to fight specific technological changes.

(b) *reform movement* -movements advocating changing some norms or laws. Examples of such a movement would include a trade union with a goal of increasing workers rights, a green movement advocating a set of ecological laws, or a movement supporting introduction of a capital punishment or the right to abortion. Some reform movements may aim for a change in custom and moral norms, such as condemnation of pornography or proliferation of some religion. innovation movement -movements which want to introduce or change particular norms, values, etc. The singularitarianism movement advocating deliberate action to effect and ensure the safety of the technological singularity is an example of an innovation movement.

3. *Methods of Work*

(a) violent movements various movements which resort to violence; they are usually armed and in extreme cases can take a form of a paramilitary or terrorist organization. Examples: the Rote Armee Fraktion, Al-Qaida.

(b) *peaceful movements:* various movements which use nonviolent means of protest. The American Civil Rights movement, Polish Solidarity movement or the nonviolent, civil disobedience-orientated wing of the Indian independence movement would fall into this category.

4. *By Targets*
   (a) *individual-focused movements:* focused on affecting individuals. Most religious movements would fall under this category.
   (b) *group-focus movements:* focused on affecting groups or society in general, for example, advocating the change of the political system. Some of these groups transform into or join a political party, but many remain outside the reformist party political system.
5. *By Time*
   (a) *old movements:* movements for change have existed for many centuries. Most of the oldest recognized movements, dating to late 18th and 19th centuries, fought for specific social groups, such as the working class, peasants, whites, aristocrats, Protestants, men. They were usually centered around some materialistic goals like improving the standard of living or, for example, the political autonomy of the working class.
   (b) *new movements:* movements which became dominant from the second half of the 20th century like the feminist movement, pro-choice movement, civil rights movement, environmental movement, free software movement, gay rights movement, peace movement, anti-nuclear movement, alter-globalization movement, etc. Sometimes they are known as new social movements. They are usually centered around issues that go beyond but are not separate from class.

6. *By Range*

   (a) *local movements:* most of the social movements have a local scope. They are focused on local or regional objectives, such as protecting a specific natural area, lobbying for the lowering of tolls in a certain motorway, or preserving a building about to be demolished for gentrification and turning it into a social center.

   (b) *global movements:* social movements with global (transnational) objectives and goals. Movements such as the first (where Marx and Bakunin met), second, third and fourth internationals, the World Social Forum, the Peoples' Global Action and the anarchist movement seek to change society at a global level.

A difficulty for scholarship of movements is that for most of them, neither insiders to a movement nor outsiders apply consistent labels or even descriptive phrases. Unless there is a single leader who does that, or a formal system of membership agreements, activists will typically use diverse labels and descriptive phrases that require scholars to discern when they are referring to the same or similar ideas, declare similar goals, adopt similar programs of action, and use similar methods. There can be great differences in the way that is done, to recognize who is and who is not a member or an allied group:

- *Insiders:* Often exaggerate the level of support by considering people supporters whose level of activity or support is weak, but also reject those that outsiders might consider supporters because they discredit the cause, or are even seen as adversaries.

- *Outsiders:* Those not supporters who may tend to either underestimate or overestimate the level or support or activity of elements of a movement, by including or excluding those that insiders would exclude or include.

In fact, it is often outsiders rather than insiders that apply the identifying labels for a movement, which the insiders then may or may not adopt and use to self-identify. For example, the label for the levellers political movement in 17th century England was applied to them by their antagonists, as a term of disparagement.

Yet admirers of the movement and its aims later came to use the term, and it is the term by which they are known to history. Caution must always be exercised in any discussion of amorphous phenomena such as movements to distinguish between the views of insiders and outsiders, supporters and antagonists, each of whom may have their own purposes and agendas in characterization or mischaracterization of it.

Dynamics of Social Movements

It is pertinent to note that social movements are not eternal. They have a life cycle: they are created, they grow, they achieve successes or failures and eventually, they dissolve and cease to exist. They are more likely to evolve in the time and place which is friendly to the social movements: hence their evident symbiosis with the 19th century proliferation of ideas like individual rights, freedom of speech and civil disobedience.

Social movements occur in liberal and authoritarian

societies but in different forms. However there must always be polarizing differences between groups of people: in case of 'old movements', they were the poverty and wealth gaps. In case of the 'new movements', they are more likely to be the differences in customs, ethics and values. Finally, the birth of a social movement needs what sociologist Neil Smelser calls an *initiating event*: a particular, individual event that will begin a chain reaction of events in the given society leading to the creation of a social movement.

For example, American Civil Rights movement grew on the reaction to black woman, Rosa Parks, riding in the whites-only section of the bus (although she was not acting alone or spontaneously—typically activist leaders lay the groundwork behind the scenes of interventions designed to spark a movement).

Similarly, the Polish Solidarity movement, which eventually toppled the communist regimes of Eastern Europe, developed after trade union activist Anna Walentynowicz was fired from work. The South African shack dwellers' movement Abahlali baseMjondolo grew out of a road blockade in response to the sudden selling off of a small piece of land promised for housing to a developer.

Such an event is also described as a *volcanic model* a social movement is often created after a large number of people realize that there are others sharing the same value and desire for a particular social change.

It is apt to mention that one of the main difficulties facing the emerging social movement is spreading the very knowledge that it exists. Second is overcoming the free rider problem convincing people to join it, instead of following the mentality 'why should I trouble myself when others can do it and I can just reap the benefits after their hard work'. Many social movements are created around some charismatic leader, i.e. one possessing charismatic authority.

After the social movement is created, there are two likely phases of recruitment. The first phase will gather the people deeply interested in the primary goal and ideal of the movement. The second phase, which will usually come after the given movement had some successes and is trendy; it would look good on a résumé. People who join in this second phase will likely be the first to leave when the movement suffers any setbacks and failures.

No exaggeration, the social crisis can be encouraged by outside elements, like opposition from government or other movements. However, many movements had survived a failure crisis, being revived by some hardcore activists even after several decades.

Main Theories

It is worthy to note here that sociologists have developed several theories related to social movements [Kendall, 2005]. Some of the better-known approaches are outlined below in the Box.

Main Approaches

- collective behavior/collective action theories (1950s)
- relative deprivation theory (1960s)
- marxist theory (1880s)
- value-added theory (1960s)
- resource mobilization (1970s)
- frame analysis theory (1980s) (closely related to social constructionist theory)
- new social movement theory (1980s)
- political process theory (1980s)

1. Deprivation Theory

Basically, deprivation theory argues that social movements have their foundations among people who feel deprived of some good(s) or resource(s). According to this approach, individuals who are lacking some good, service, or comfort are more likely to organize a social movement to improve (or defend) their conditions. There are two significant problems with this theory.

First, since most people feel deprived at one level or another almost all the time, the theory has a hard time explaining why the groups that form social movements do when other people are also deprived.

Second, the reasoning behind this theory is circular often the only evidence for deprivation is the social movement. If deprivation is claimed to be the cause but the only evidence for such is the movement, the reasoning is circular.

2. Mass Society Theory

mass society theory argues that social movements are made up of individuals in large societies who feel insignificant or socially detached. Social movements, according to this theory, provide a sense of empowerment and belonging that the movement members would otherwise not have.

Notably, very little support has been found for this theory. Aho (1990), in his study of Idaho Christian Patriotism, did not find that members of that movement were more likely to have been socially detached. In fact, the key to joining the movement was having a friend or associate who was a member of the movement.

3. Marxist Theory

Basically, derived from Karl Marx, Marxism as an ideology and theory of social change has had an immense impact on the practice and the analysis of social movements. Marxism arose from an analysis of movements structured by conflicts between industrial workers and their capitalist employers in the 19th century. In the twentieth century a variety of neo-Marxist theories have been developed that have opened themselves to adding questions of race, gender, environment, and other issues to an analysis centered in (shifting) political economic conditions.

Class-based movements, both revolutionary and labor-reformist, have always been stronger in Europe than in the US and so has Marxist theory as a tool for understanding social movements, but important Marxist movements and theories have also evolved in the US. Marxist approaches have been and remain influential ways of understanding the role of political economy and class differences as key forces in many historical and current social movements, and they continue to challenge approaches that are limited by their inability to imagine serious alternatives to consumer capitalist social structures.

4. Structural Strain Theory

It is pertinent to note that structural strain theory proposes six factors that encourage social movement development:

1. structural conduciveness people come to believe their society has problems
2. structural strain people experience deprivation
3. growth and spread of a solution a solution to the problems people are experiencing is proposed and spreads
4. precipitating factors discontent usually requires a catalyst (often a specific event) to turn it into a social movement

5. mobilization this is the actual organizing and active component of the movement; people do what needs to be done
6. lack of social control the entity that is to be changed must be at least somewhat open to the change; if the social movement is quickly and powerfully repressed, it may never materialize

It must be remembered that this theory is also subject to circular reasoning as it incorporates, at least in part, deprivation theory and relies upon it, and social/structural strain for the underlying motivation of social movement activism. However, social movement activism is, like in the case of deprivation theory, often the only indication that there was strain or deprivation.

5. Resource Mobilization Theory

Basically, resource mobilization theory emphasizes the importance of resources in social movement development and success. Resources are understood here to include: knowledge, money, media, labor, solidarity, legitimacy, and internal and external support from power elite. The theory argues that social movements develop when individuals with grievances are able to mobilize sufficient resources to take action.

The emphasis on resources offers an explanation why some discontented/deprived individuals are able to organize while others are not.

Following may be some of the assumptions of the theory:

(a) actors are rational; they weigh the costs and benefits from movement participation

(b) there will always be grounds for protest in modern,

politically pluralistic societies because there is constant discontent (i.e., grievances or deprivation); this de-emphasizes the importance of these factors as it makes them ubiquitous

(c) members are recruited through networks; commitment is maintained by building a collective identity and continuing to nurture interpersonal relationships

(d) social movement organizations require resources and continuity of leadership

(e) movement organization is contingent upon the aggregation of resources

(f) the form of the resources shapes the activities of the movement (e.g., access to a TV station will result in the extensive use of TV media)

(g) social movement entrepreneurs and protest organizations are the catalysts which transform collective discontent into social movements; social movement organizations form the *backbone* of social movements

(h) movements develop in contingent *opportunity structures* that influence their efforts to mobilize; as each movement's response to the opportunity structures depends on the movement's organization and resources, there is no clear pattern of movement development nor are specific movement techniques or methods universal.

It is pertinent to note that critics of this theory argue that there is too much of an emphasize on resources, especially financial resources. Some movements are effective without an influx of money and are more dependent upon the movement members for time and labor.

6. Culture Theory

It is apt to mention that more recent strains of theory understand social movements through their cultures collectively shared beliefs, ideologies, values and other meanings about the world. These include explorations into the "collective identities" and "collective action frames" of movements and movement organizations.

Basically, culture theory builds upon both the political process and resource-mobilization theories but extends them in two ways.

First, it emphasizes the importance of movement culture. Second, it attempts to address the free-rider problem. Both resource-mobilization theory and political process theory include a sense of injustice in their approaches. Culture theory brings this sense of injustice to the forefront of movement creation by arguing that, in order for social movements to successfully mobilize individuals, they must develop an *injustice frame.*

An injustice frame is a collection of ideas and symbols that illustrate both how significant the problem is as well as what the movement can do to alleviate it, "Like a picture frame, an issue frame marks off some part of the world. Like a building frame, it holds things together. It provides coherence to an array of symbols, images, and arguments, linking them through an underlying organizing idea that suggests what is essential what consequences and values are at stake. We do not see the frame directly, but infer its presence by its characteristic expressions and language. Each frame gives the advantage to certain ways of talking and thinking, while it places others out of the picture."

7. Political Process Theory

Political process theory is similar to resource mobilization in many regards, but tends to emphasize a different component of social structure that is important for social movement development: political opportunities.

Political process theory argues that there are three vital components for movement formation: insurgent consciousness, organizational strength, and political opportunities. Insurgent consciousness refers back to the ideas of deprivation and grievances. The idea is that certain members of society feel like they are being mistreated or that somehow the system is unjust. The insurgent consciousness is the collective sense of injustice that movement members (or potential movement members) feel and serves as the motivation for movement organization.

In fact, organizational strength falls inline with resource-mobilization theory, arguing that in order for a social movement to organize it must have strong leadership and sufficient resources. Political opportunity refers to the receptivity or vulnerability of the existing political system to challenge. This vulnerability can be the result of any of the following:

- growth of political pluralism
- decline in effectiveness of repression
- elite disunity; the leading factions are internally fragmented
- a broadening of access to institutional participation in political processes
- support of organized opposition by elites

In fact, one of the advantages of the political process theory is that it addresses the issue of timing or emergence of social movements. Some groups may have the insurgent consciousness and resources to mobilize, but because political opportunities are closed, they will not have any success. The theory, then, argues that all three of these components are important. Critics of the political process theory and resource-mobilization theory point out that neither theory discusses movement culture to any great degree. This has presented culture theorists an opportunity to expound on the importance of culture. One advance on the political process theory is the *political mediation model,* which outlines the way in which the political context facing movement actors intersects with the strategic choices that movements make.

An additional strength of this model is that it can look at the outcomes of social movements not only in terms of success or failure but also in terms of consequences (whether intentional or unintentional, positive or negative) and in terms of collective benefits.

Important Characteristics

- Facts take on their meaning by being embedded in frames, which render them relevant and significant or irrelevant and trivial.
- People carry around multiple frames in their heads.
- Successful reframing involves the ability to enter into the worldview of our adversaries.
- All frames contain implicit or explicit appeals to moral principles.

In fact, culture theory also addresses the free-rider problem in emphasizing the injustice frame. The free-rider problem refers to the idea that people will not be motivated to participate in a social movement that will use up their personal resources (e.g., time, money, etc.) if they can still receive the benefits without participating. In other words, if person X knows that movement Y is working to improve health conditions in his neighborhood, he is presented with a choice: join or not join the movement. If he believes the movement will succeed without him, he can avoid participation in the movement, save his resources, and still reap the benefits - this is *free-riding*.

A significant problem for social movement theory has been to explain why people join movements if they believe the movement can/will succeed without their contribution. Culture theory argues that, in conjunction with social networks being an important contact tool, the injustice frame will provide the motivation for people to contribute to the movement.

Components of Framing Processes

(a) Diagnostic frame: the movement organization frames what is the problem or what they are critiquing

(b) Prognostic frame: the movement organization frames what is the desirable solution to the problem

(c) Motivational frame: the movement organization frames a "call to arms" by suggesting and encouraging that people take action to solve the problem.

It is apt to mention that much discussion has been generated recently on the topic of social networking and the effect it may play on the formation and mobilization of social movement. For example, the emergence of the Coffee Party first appeared on the social networking site, Facebook. The party has continued to gather membership and support through that site and file sharing sites, such as Flickr. The 2009–2010 Iranian election protests also demonstrated how social networking sites are making the mobilization of large numbers of people quicker and easier. Iranians were able to organize and speak out against the election of Mahmoud Ahmadinejad by using sites such as Twitter and Facebook.

REFERENCES

Anthony Giddens. 1985. *The Nation-State and Violence.* Cambridge, England: Polity Press.

Armand L. Mauss. 1975. Social Problems of Social Movements. Philadelphia: Lippincott.

Charles Tilly, *Social Movements, 1768–2004*, Boulder, CO, Paradigm Publishers, 2004.

Charlotte Ryan and William W. Gamson, The Art of Reframing Political Debates. *Contexts.* 2006; 5(1):13-18.

David F. Aberle 1966. *The Peyote Religion among the Navaho.* Chicago: Aldine.

David Snow, Sarah A. Soule and Hanspeter Kriesi, ed. *Blackwell Companion to Social Movements,* Blackwell, 2004.

Denton E. Morrison. 1978. "Some Notes toward Theory on Relative Deprivation, Social Movements, and Social Change." In Louis E. Genevie, ed., *Collective Behavior and Social Movements.* Itasca, Ill.: Peacock. pp. 202–209.

Diana Kendall, *Sociology In Our Times*, Thomson Wadsworth, 2005.

Diani, Mario, and Doug McAdam. Social movements and networks. Oxford University Press, 2003.

Donna Maurer. 2002. *Vegetarianism: Movement or Moment?* Philadelphia: Temple University Press.

Graeme Chesters, & Ian Welsh. *Complexity and Social Movements: Multitudes at the Edge of Chaos* Routledge 2006.

Herbert G. Blumer 1969. "Collective Behavior." In Alfred McClung Lee, ed., Principles of Sociology. Third Edition. New York: Barnes and Noble Books, pp. 65–121.

Immanuel Ness, ed. *Encyclopedia of American Social Movements,* 2004.

J. Craig Jenkins and Charles Perrow. 1977. Insurgency of the Powerless Farm Worker Movements (1946–1972). American Sociological Review. 42(2):249-268.

James Alfred Aho. 1990. *Politics of Righteousness: Idaho Christian Patriotism.* Washington: University of Washington Press.

Mark Chaves. 1997. *Ordaining Women: Culture and Conflict in Religious Organizations.* Cambridge: Harvard University Press.

Sidney Tarrow, *Power in Movement: Collective Action, Social Movements and Politics*, Cambridge University Press, 1994.

Smelser, Neil J. 1962. *Theory of Collective Behavior.* New York: Free Press.

Susan Eckstei, ed. *Power and Popular Protest: Latin American Social Movements*, Updated Edition, University of California Press 2001.

Suzanne Staggenborg, *Social Movements*, Oxford University Press, 2008.

Tilly, Charles. 1978. *From Mobilization to Revolution.* Reading, Massachusetts: Addison-Wesley, 1978.

William Kornhauser. 1959. *The Politics of Mass Society.* New York: Free Press.

3

Social Movements In India

It is pertinent to note that Social Movement is one of the major forms of collective behaviour.We hear of various kinds of social movements launched for one or the other purpose. A social movement can be defined as collectively acing with some continuity to promote or resist change in the society or group of which it is a part.

Horton and Hunt have defined it as a collective effort to promote or resist change.Smelser defines it as organized group effort to generate or resist social change. According to M.S.A Rao social movement includes two characteristics.

Social Movement involves collective action. However it takes the form of a movement only when it is sustained for a long time. This collective action need not be formally organized. But it should be able to create an interest and awakening in relatively large number of people.

A social movement is generally oriented towards bringing social change. This change could either be partial or total. Though the movement is aimed at bringing about a change in the values, norms, ideologies of the existing system, efforts are also made by some other forces to resist the changes and to maintain the status quo.The counter attempts are normally defensive and restorative rather than innovative and initiating change. They are normally the organized efforts of an already established order to maintain itself.

According to Yogendra Singh social movement is a collective mobilization of people in a society in an organized manner under an individual or collective leadership in order to realize an ideologically defined social purpose. Social movements are characterized by a specific goal which has a collective significance ideological interpretation of the collective goal a rank of committed worker and strong leadership.Social movements have a life-cycle of their own origin, maturity and culmination.T.K Oomen observe that a study of social movements implies a study of social structure as movements originate from the contradictions which in turn emanate from social structure. He states that all social movements centre around three factors- Locality, Issues and social categories. Anthony Wallace view social movement as an attempt by local population to change the image or models they have of how their culture operates.

An important component of social movement that distinguishes it from the general category of collective mobilization is the presence of an ideology. A student strike involves collective mobilization and is oriented towards change. But in the absence of an ideology a student strike becomes an isolated event and not a movement. A social movement requires a minimum of organizational framework to achieve success or at least to maintain the tempo of the movement. To make the distinction clear between the leaders and followers to make clear the purposes of the movement to persuade people to take part in it or to support it, to adopt different techniques to achieve the goals - a social movement must have some amount of organizational framework. A social movement may adopt its own technique or method to achieve its goal. It may follow peaceful or conflicting, violent or non-violent, compulsive or persuasive, democratic or undemocratic means or methods to reach its goal.

Main Types of Social Movements

1. Reform Movements: Reform movements are organized to carry out reforms in some specific areas. The reformers endeavor to change elements of the system for better. For example: Civil Rights Movement, Women's Liberation Movement, Arya Samaj Movement, Brahmo Samaj Movement etc.

2. Revolutionary Movements: The revolutionary movements deny that the system will even work. These movements are deeply dissatisfied with the social order and work for radical change. They advocate replacing the entire existing structure. Their objective is the reorganization of society in accordance with their own ideological blueprint. Revolutionary movements generally become violent as they progress. Example: The Protestant Reformation Movement, the Socialist Movement, the Communist Revolution of China.

3. Resistance Movement: These movements are formed to resist a change that is already taking place in society. These can be directed against social and cultural changes which are already happening in the country.

4. Utopian Movement: These are attempts to take the society or a section of it towards a state of perfection. These are loosely structured collectivities that envision a radically changed and blissful state, either on a large scale at some time in the future or on a smaller scale in the present. The Utopian ideal and the means of it are often vague, but many utopian movements have quite specific programmes for social change. The Hare Krishna Movement of the seventies, the movement towards the establishment of Ram Rajya and the Sangh Parivar, the Communists and Socialists pronouncement of a movement towards the classless, casteless society free from all kinds of exploitation etc.

5. Reactionary or Revivalist Movement: Some movements are known as reactionary or regressive movements. These aims to reverse the social change .They highlight the importance and greatness of traditional values, ideologies and institutional arrangements. They strongly criticize the fast moving changes of the present.

6. Peasant Movement : Peasant movement is defined by Kathleen Gough as an attempt of a group to effect change in the face of resistance and the peasant are people who are engaged in an agricultural or related production with primitive means who surrender part of their or its equivalent to landlords or to agents of change.

The history of peasant movements can be traced to colonial period when repressive economic policies, the new land revenue system, the colonial administrative and judicial system and the ruin of handicrafts leading to the overcrowding of land transformed the agrarian structure and impoverished the peasantry. In the zamindari system peasants were left to the mercies of the Zamindars who exploited them in form of illegal dues.

The British government levied heavy land revenue in the Ryotwari areas. Peasants were forced to borrow money from the moneylenders and they were reduced to the status of tenants at will, share croppers and landless laborers while their lands, crops and cattle passed into the hands to landlords, trader moneylenders and such peasants. When the peasants could take it no longer they resisted against the oppression and exploitation through uprisings.

Peasant Movements occupy an important place in the history of social unrest in India though the aims and objectives of these movements differ in nature and degree from region to region. It is in this sense that these movements also aimed at the unification of the peasants of a region, development of leadership, ideology and a peasant elite.

Through these movements emerged a new power structure and peasant alliance. The genesis of peasant movements rest in the relationship patterns of different social categories existing within the framework of feudal and semi feudal structure of our society. In the post Independence period the nature and objectives of the peasant movement have changed to getting remunerative prices for agricultural produce, to increase agricultural production, to establish parity between prices of agricultural produce and industrial goods and to get minimum wages for the agricultural laborers.

Important Peasant Uprising in India

1770- Sanyasi rebellion

1831- Wahabi uprising

1855- Santhal uprising

1859- Indigo revolt

1890-1900- Punjab Kisan struggle

1917-18- Champaran satyagraha

1921- Moplah rebellion

1928- Bardoli satyagarya

1946- Telangana movement

1957- Naxalbai movement

Women's Movement

The women's movement in India is a rich and vibrant

movement which has taken different forms in different parts of the country. Fifty years ago when India became independent, it was widely acknowledged that the battle for freedom had been fought as much by women as by men. One of the methods M K Gandhi chose to undermine the authority of the British was for Indians to defy the law which made it illegal for them to make salt. At the time, salt-making was a monopoly and earned considerable revenues for the British. Gandhi began his campaign by going on a march - the salt march - through many villages, leading finally to the sea, where he and others broke the law by making salt. No woman had been included by Gandhi in his chosen number of marchers. But nationalist women protested, and they forced him to allow them to participate. The first to join was Sarojini Naidu, who went on to become the first woman President of the Indian National Congress in 1925. Her presence was a signal for hundreds of other women to join, and eventually the salt protest was made successful by the many women who not only made salt, but also sat openly in marketplaces selling, and indeed, buying it.

The trajectory of this movement is usually traced from the social reform movements of the 19th century when campaigns for the betterment of the conditions of women's lives were taken up, initially by men. By the end of the century women had begun to organize themselves and gradually they took up a number of causes such as education, the conditions of women's work and so on. It was in the early part of the 20th century that women's organizations were set up, and many of the women who were active in these later became involved in the freedom movement. Independence brought many promises and dreams for women in India - the dream of an egalitarian, just, democratic society in which both men and women would have a voice.

The reality was, however, somewhat different. For all that had happened was that, despite some improvements in the status of women, patriarchy had simply taken on new and different forms. By the 1960s it was clear that many of the promises of Independence were still unfulfilled. It was thus that the 1960s and 1970s saw a spate of movements in which women took part: campaigns against rising prices, movements for land rights, peasant movements. Women from different parts of the country came together to form groups both inside and outside political parties. Everywhere, in the different movements that were sweeping the country, women participated in large numbers. Everywhere, their participation resulted in transforming the movements from within. One of the first issues to receive countrywide attention from women's groups was violence against women, specifically in the form of rape, and 'dowry deaths'. This was also the beginning of a process of learning for women: most protests were directed at the State.

Because women were able to mobilize support, the State responded, seemingly positively, by changing the law on rape and dowry, making both more stringent. In the early campaigns, groups learnt from day to day that targeting the State was not enough and that victims also needed support. So a further level of work was needed: awareness raising so that violence against women could be prevented, rather than only dealt with after it had happened. Legal aid and counseling centres were set up, and attempts were made to establish women's shelters.

Knowledge was also recognized as an important need. The women's activity was geared towards improving the conditions of women's lives. In recent years, the euphoria of the 1970s and early 1980s, symbolized by street-level protests, campaigns in which groups mobilized at a national level, has been replaced by a more considered and complex response to issues. In many parts of India, women are no longer to be seen out on the streets protesting about this or that form of injustice.

This apparent lack of a visible movement has led to the accusation that the women's movement is dead or dying. While the participation of urban, middle class women is undeniable, it is not they who make up the backbone of the movement, or of the many, different campaigns that are generally seen as comprising the movement. The anti-alcohol agitation in Andhra Pradesh and similar campaigns in other parts of India were started and sustained by poor, low-caste, often working-class women.

The movement to protect the environment was begun by poor women in a village called Reni in the northern hill regions of India, and only after that did it spread to other parts of the country. One of the biggest challenges women have had to face in recent years is the growing influence of the religious right in India. Right-wing groups have built much of their support on the involvement of women: offering to help them with domestic problems, enabling them to enter the public space in a limited way, and all the while ensuring that the overall ideology within which they operate remains firmly patriarchal.

For activists too, this has posed major problems. It has forced them to confront the fact that they cannot assume solidarity as women that cuts across class, religion, caste, ethnic difference. It is important to recognize that for a country of India's magnitude, change in male-female relations and the kinds of issues the women's movement is focusing on will not come easy. For every step the movement takes forward, there will be a possible backlash, a possible regression.

And it is this that makes for the contradictions, this that makes it possible for there to be women who can aspire to, and attain, the highest political office in the country, and for women to continue to have to confront patriarchy within the home, in the workplace, throughout their lives.

Backward Caste Movement

It must be remembered that Backward castes have been deprived of many social, economic, political and religious privileges. These people provided manual labor and the untouchables occupied the lowest position among the caste hierarchy. They were subjected to extreme form of exploitation. The colonial power accentuated the disparities in the distribution of economic power. The atrocities united the lower castes against the upper castes. Some of the important backward caste movement which came up was Satyashodak Samaj and Nadar Movement which consolidated the masses along the castelines.

E.V Ramaswamy started Self-Respect movement against the Brahmins in South India. The SNDP movement in Kerala was more of a reformist movement. In 1950s there was a widespread desire among the non-Brahmin castes to be categorized as Backward .Subsequently Backward Class commission was set up to look into the conditions and requirements of these classes. Mandal Commission submitted its report in 1980 recommending reservations for backward castes in educational institutions and government offices. However this move resulted in anti-Mandal Commission movement which resulted in large scale violence and many students lost their lives.

Dalit Movement

Dalits are the suppressed people at the lowest rung of the caste-based hierarchy. Their inferior occupations and low levels of ascriptive status make them vulnerable for attacks at the hands of upper-caste people. The organizational efforts made by Dalit leadership for uplifting their status are known as Dalit movement. It is a protest against untouchability ,casteism and discrimination faced by the dalits.Dalit movement indicates some trends of protest ideologies which entail the following -withdrawal and self organization, high varna status and extolling of non-Aryan culture's virtues, abandoning of Hinduism and embracing other religions like Buddhism and Islam. Mahatma Gandhi in 1923 founded the All India Harijan Sevak Sangh to start education and schools for the dalits.Another most important dalit leader Dr.Ambedkar struggled to secure the basic human dignity to the dalits.The Mahad Satyagarh for the right of water led by him was one of the outstanding movements of the dalits to win equal social rights. The role of All India Depressed Classes Association and All India Depressed Classes Federation were the principal organizations which initiated a movement to improve the conditions of the dalits.These organizations aimed at improving their miserable conditions and to spread education among them. They worked to secure rights of admission to school, drawing water from the public wells, entering the temples and to use the roads.

4

Role of Social Change

The term social change is used to indicate the changes that take place in human interactions and interrelations. Society is a web of social relationships and hence social change means change in the system of social relationships. These are understood in terms of social processes and social interactions and social organization.Auguste Comte the father of Sociology has posed two problems- the question of social statics and the question of social dynamics, what is and how it changes. The sociologists not only outline the structure of the society but also seek to know its causes also. According to Morris Ginsberg social change is a change in the social structure.

Important Points

1. Social change that occurs without being noticed by most members is called latent change.
2. Walter Cannon coined the term Homeostasis.
3. David Glass conducted the first study of inter-generational mobility in England and Wales.
4. To Pitrim Sorokin societies pass through three stages each dominated by a system of truth. The stages are ideational, sensate, idealistic .This theory is the example of cyclical theory.

5. To Herbert Spencer mankind had progressed from small groups to large and from simple to compound and doubly compound or in more general terms from the homogenous to the heterogeneous. This conception is an example of linear theory.
6. Giddings formulated a law of social change .He founded neo-positivist school.
7. Marx and Engels put forward a materialist variant of the evolutionary theory.
8. Herbert Spencer propounded the theory of social evolution.
9. M.N Srinivas wrote the famous book social change in modern India.
11. Goffmann regards total institutions as forcing houses for changing persons.
12. Sorokin has written social and cultural dynamics.
13. The notion of order, change and progress are inherent in the concept of evolution.
14. Maine argued that societies developed from organizational forms where relationships were based on status to those based upon contract.
15. Saint Simon distinguished between three stages of mental activity- The conjectural, unconjectural and positive.
16. Cities and towns came into existence due to development of commerce.
17. Ogburn introduced the concept of cultural lag in his book Social Change.
18. According to Lester F Ward social change can be bought about by means of conscious and systematic effort.
19. David Aberle has classified social movements as transformative, reformative, redemptive and alternative.
20. Stouffer is associated wit h the theory of relative deprivation.

21. According to Toffler technology would bring about a reversal of trend towards mass culture distributed by television.
22. Clark Kerr is the author of convergence theory.
23. Everett Rogers categorized people as innovators, early adopter and larggerds on basis of their response to an innovation.
24. Tonnies proposed that human societies evolve from communities bound together by tradition to those characterized by nonemotional objectivity.
25. Sorokin is associated with the theory of variable recurrence.
26. Dalit Panther Movement emerged among Mahars.
27. Dalit Panther Movement is transformative movement.

Evolutionary Theories

Evolutionary theories are based on the assumption that societies gradually change from simple beginnings into even more complex forms. Early sociologists beginning with Auguste Comte believed that human societies evolve in a unilinear way- that is in one line of development. According to them social change meant progress toward something better. They saw change as positive and beneficial. To them the evolutionary process implied that societies would necessarily reach new and higher levels of civilization.L.H Morgan believed that there were three basic stages in the process: savagery, barbarism and civilization.Auguste Comte's ideas relating to the three stages in the development of human thought and also of society namely-the theological, the metaphysical and the positive in a way represent the three basic stages of social change. This evolutionary view of social change was highly influenced by Charles Darwin's theory of Organic Evolution.

Those who were fascinated by this theory applied it to the human society and argued that societies must have evolved from the simple and primitive to that of too complex and advanced such as the western society. Herbert Spencer a British sociologist carried this analogy to its extremity. He argued that society itself is an organism. He even applied Darwin's principle of the survival of the fittest to human societies. He said that society has been gradually progressing towards a better state. He argued that it has evolved from military society to the industrial society. He claimed that western races, classes or societies had survived and evolved because they were better adapted to face the conditions of life.

This view known as social Darwinism got widespread popularity in the late 19th century. It survived even during the first phase of the 20th century. Emile Durkheim identified the cause of societal evolution as a society's increasing moral density.Durkheim viewed societies as changing in the direction of greater differentiation, interdependence and formal control under the pressure of increasing moral density. He advocated that societies have evolved from a relatively undifferentiated social structure with minimum of division of labor and with a kind of solidarity called mechanical solidarity to a more differentiated social structure with maximum division of labor giving rise to a kind of solidarity called organic solidarity.

Cyclical Theories

Cyclical theories of social change focus on the rise and fall of civilizations attempting to discover and account for these patterns of growth and decay.Spengler, Toynbee and Sorokin can be regarded as the champions of this theory.Spengler pointed out that the fate of civilizations was a matter of destiny. Each civilization is like a biological organism and has a similar life-cycle, birth, maturity, old-age and death.

After making a study of eight major civilizations including the west he said that the modern western society is in the last stage i.e. old age. He concluded that the western societies were entering a period of decay as evidenced by wars, conflicts and social breakdown that heralded their doom.

Arnold Toynbee's famous book *'A study of History'* (1946) focus on the key concepts of challenge and response. Every society faces challenges at first, challenges posed by the environment and later challenges from internal and external enemies. The nature of responses determines the society's fate. The achievements of a civilization consist of its successful responses to the challenges; if cannot mount an effective response it dies. He does not believe that all civilizations will inevitably decay. He has pointed out that history is a series of cycles of decay and growth. But each new civilization is able to learn from the mistakes and to borrow from cultures of others. It is therefore possible for each new cycle to offer higher level of achievement.

Pitirin Sorokin in his book *Social and Culture Dynamics* (1938) has offered another explanation of social change. Instead of viewing civilization into the terms of development and decline he proposed that they alternate of fluctuate between two cultural extremes: the sensate and the ideational. The sensate culture stresses those things which can be perceived directly by the senses. It is practical, hedonistic, sensual and materialistic.

Ideational culture emphasizes those things which can be perceived only by the mind. It is abstract, religious concerned with faith and ultimate truth. It is the opposite of the sensate culture. Both represent pure types of culture. Hence no society ever fully conforms to either type. As the culture of a society develops towards one pure type, it is countered by the opposing cultural force. Cultural development is then reversed moving towards the opposite type of culture. Too much emphasis on one type of culture leads to a reaction towards the other. Societies contain both these impulses in varying degrees and the tension between them creates long-term instability. Between these types lies a third type 'idealistic' culture. This is a desirable blend of other two but no society ever seems to have achieved it as a stable condition.

Functionalist or Dynamic Theories

In the middle decades of the 20th century a number of American sociologists shifted their attention from social dynamics to social static or from social change to social stability.Talcott Parsons stressed the importance of cultural patterns in controlling the stability of a society. According to him society has the ability to absorb disruptive forces while maintaining overall stability. Change is not as something that disturbs the social equilibrium but as something that alters the state of equilibrium so that a qualitatively new equilibrium results. He has stated that changes may arise from two sources. They may come from outside the society through contact with other societies. They may also come from inside the society through adjustment that must be made to resolve strains within the system. Parsons speaks of two processes that are at work in social change. In simple societies institutions are undifferentiated that is a single institution serves many functions. The family performs reproductive, educational, socializing, economic, recreational and other functions. A process of differentiation takes place when the society becomes more and more complex. Different institutions such as school, factory may take over some of the functions of a family. The new institutions must be linked together in a proper way by the process of integration. New norms must be established in order to govern the relationship between the school and the home. Further bridging institutions such as law courts must resolve conflicts between other components in the system.

Conflict Theories

Whereas the equilibrium theories emphasize the stabilizing processes at work in social systems the so-called conflict theories highlight the forces producing instability, struggle and social disorganization. According to Ralf Dahrendorf the conflict theories assume that - every society is subjected at every moment to change, hence social change is ubiquitous. Every society experiences at every moment social conflict, hence social conflict is ubiquitous. Every element in society contributes to change. Every society rests on constraint of some of its members by others. The most famous and influential of the conflict theories is the one put forward by Karl Marx who along with Engel wrote in Communist Manifesto 'all history is the history of class conflict.' Individuals and groups with opposing interests are bound to be at conflict. Since the two major social classes the rich and poor or capitalists and the proletariat have mutually hostile interests they are at conflict. History is the story of conflict between the exploiter and the exploited. This conflict repeats itself off and on until capitalism is overthrown by the workers and a socialist state is created. What is to be stressed here is that Marx and other conflict theorists deem society as basically dynamic and not static. They consider conflict as a normal process. They also believe that the existing conditions in any society contain the seeds of future social changes. Like Karl Marx George Simmel too stressed the importance of conflict in social change. According to him conflict is a permanent feature of society and not just a temporary event. It is a process that binds people together in interaction. Further conflict encourages people of similar interests to unite together to achieve their objectives. Continuous conflict in this way keeps society dynamic and ever changing.

Factors of Change

Physical Environment

Major changes in the physical environment are very compelling when they happen. The desert wastes of North Africa were once green and well populated. Climates change, soil erodes and lakes gradually turn into swamps and finally plains. A culture is greatly affected by such changes although sometimes they come about so slowly that they are largely unnoticed. Human misuse can bring very rapid changes in physical environment which in turn change the social and cultural life of a people. Deforestation brings land erosion and reduces rainfall. Much of the wasteland and desert land of the world is a testament to human ignorance and misuse. Environmental destruction has been at least a contributing factor in the fall of most great civilization. Many human groups throughout history have changed their physical environment through migration. In the primitive societies whose members are very directly dependent upon their physical environment migration to a different environment brings major changes in the culture. Civilization makes it easy to transport a culture and practice it in a new and different environment.

Population Changes

A population change is itself a social change but also

becomes a casual factor in further social and cultural changes. When a thinly settled frontier fills up with people the hospitality pattern fades away, secondary group relations multiply, institutional structures grow more elaborate and many other changes follow. A stable population may be able to resist change but a rapidly growing population must migrate, improve its productivity or starve. Great historic migrations and conquests of the Huns, Vikings and many others have arisen from the pressure of a growing population upon limited resources.

Migration encourages further change for it brings a group into a new environment subjects it to new social contacts and confronts it with new problems. No major population change leaves the culture unchanged.

Isolation and Contact

Societies located at world crossroads have always been centers of change. Since most new traits come through diffusion, those societies in closest contact with other societies are likely to change most rapidly. In ancient times of overland transport, the land bridge connecting Asia, Africa and Europe was the centre of civilizing change.

Later sailing vessels shifted the centre to the fringes of the Mediterranean Sea and still later to the north- west coast of Europe. Areas of greatest intercultural contact are the centers of change. War and trade have always brought intercultural contact and today tourism is adding to the contacts between cultures says Greenwood.

Conversely isolated areas are centers of stability, conservatism and resistance to change. The most primitive tribes have been those who were the most isolated like the polar Eskimos or the Aranda of Central Australia.

Social Structure

The structure of a society affects its rate of change in subtle and not immediately apparent ways. A society which vests great authority in the very old people as classical China did for centuries is likely to be conservative and stable. According to Ottenberg a society which stresses conformity and trains the individual to be highly responsive to the group such as the Zunis is less receptive to the change than a society like the Ileo who are highly individualistic and tolerate considerable cultural variability.

A highly centralized bureaucracy is very favorable to the promotion and diffusion of change although bureaucracy has sometimes been used in an attempt to suppress change usually with no more than temporary success. When a culture is very highly integrated so that each element is rightly interwoven with all the others in a mutually interdependent system change is difficult and costly. But when the culture is less highly integrated so that work, play, family, religion and other activities are less dependent upon one another change is easier and more frequent.

A tightly structured society wherein every person's roles, duties, privileges and obligations are precisely and rigidly defined is less given to changes than a more loosely structured society wherein roles, lines of authority, privileges and obligations are more open to individual rearrangement.

Attitudes and Values

To people in developed nations and societies change is normal. Children there are socialized to anticipate and appreciate change. By contrast the Trobriand Islanders off the coast of New Guinea had no concept of change and did not even have any words in their language to express or describe change. Societies differ greatly in their general attitude toward change. People who revere the past and preoccupied with traditions and rituals will change slowly and unwillingly. When a culture has been relatively static for a long time the people are likely to assume that it should remain so indefinitely. They are intensely and unconsciously ethnocentric; they assume that their customs and techniques are correct and everlasting. A possible change is unlikely even to be seriously considered. Any change in such a society is likely to be too gradual to be noticed. A rapidly changing society has a different attitude toward change and this attitude is both cause and effect of the changes already taking place. Rapidly changing societies are aware of the social change. They are somewhat skeptical and critical of some parts of their traditional culture and will consider and experiment with innovations. Such attitudes powerfully stimulate the proposal and acceptance of changes by individuals within the society. Different groups within a locality or a society may show differing receptivity to change.

Every changing society has its liberals and its conservatives. Literate and educated people tend to accept changes more readily than the illiterate and uneducated. Attitudes and values affect both the amount and the direction of social change. The ancient Greeks made great contributions to art and learning but contributed little to technology. No society has been equally dynamic in all aspects and its values determine in which area-art, music, warfare, technology, philosophy or religion it will be innovative.

In fact, cultural factor influences the direction and character of technological change Culture not only influences our social relationships, it also influences the direction and character of technological change. It is not only our beliefs and social institutions must correspond to the changes in technology but our beliefs and social institutions determine the use to which the technological inventions will be put.

The tools and techniques of technology are indifferent to the use we make of them. For example the atomic energy can be used for the production of deadly war weapons or for the production of economic goods that satisfy the basic needs of man. The factories can produce the armaments or necessaries of life. Steel and iron can be used for building warships or tractors. It is a culture that decides the purpose to which a technical invention must be put. Although technology has advanced geometrically in the recent past, technology alone does not cause social change. It does not by itself even cause further advances in technology. Social values play a dominant role here.

It is the complex combination of technology and social values which produces conditions that encourage further technological change. For example the belief or the idea that human life must not be sacrificed for wants of medical treatment, contributed to the advancement in medical technology.

Max Weber in his *The Protestant Ethic and the spirit of Capitalism* has made a classical attempt to establish a correlation between the changes in the religious outlook, beliefs and practices of the people on the one hand and their economic behavior on the other. He has observed capitalism could grow in the western societies to very great extent and not in the eastern countries like India and China. He has concluded that Protestantism with its practical ethics encouraged capitalism to grow in the west and hence industrial and economic advancement took place there.

In the East, Hinduism, Buddhism, Judaism and Islam on the other hand did not encourage capitalism. Thus cultural factors play a positive as well as negative role in bringing about technological change.

Cultural factors such as habits, customs, traditions, conservatism, traditional values etc may resist the technological inventions. On the other hand factors such as breakdown in the unity of social values, the diversification of social institutions craving for the new thoughts, values etc may contribute to technological inventions. Technological changes do not take place on their own. They are engineered by men only.

Technology is the creation of man. Men are always moved by ideas, thoughts, values, beliefs, morals and philosophies etc.These are the elements of culture. These sometimes decide or influence the direction in which technology undergoes change.

Men are becoming more and more materialistic in their attitude. This change in the attitude and outlook is reflected in the technological field. Thus in order to lead a comfortable life and to minimize the manual labor man started inventing new techniques, machines, instruments and devices.

Technological Factors

The technological factors represent the conditions created by man which have a profound influence on his life. In the attempt to satisfy his wants, fulfill his needs and to make his life more comfortable man creates civilization. Technology is a byproduct of civilization .When the scientific knowledge is applied to the problems in life it becomes technology. Technology is a systematic knowledge which is put into practice that is to use tools and run machines to serve human purpose. Science and technology go together. In utilizing the products of technology man brings social change. The social effects of technology are far-reaching. According to Karl Marx even the formation of social relations and mental conceptions and attitudes are dependent upon technology. He has regarded technology as a sole explanation of social change.W.F Ogburn says technology changes society by changing our environment to which we in turn adapt. These changes are usually in the material environment and the adjustment that we make with these changes often modifies customs and social institutions. A single invention may have innumerable social effects. Radio for example has One of the most extreme expressions of the concern over the independence of technology is found in Jacques Ellul's 'the technological society'. Ellul claims that in modern industrial societies technologism has engulfed every aspect of social existence in much the same way Catholicism did in the middle ages. The loss of human freedom and the large-scale destruction of human beings are due to the increasing use of certain types of technology which has begun to threaten the life support systems of the earth as a whole.

Impact of Technology Change

Technology has contributed to the growth of industries or to the process of industrialization. Industrialization is a term covering in general terms the growth in a society hitherto mainly agrarian of modern industry with all its circumstances and problems, economic and social. It describes in general term the growth of a society in which a major role is played by manufacturing industry. The industry is characterized by heavy, fixed capital investment in plant and building by the application of science to industrial techniques and by mainly large-scale standardized production. The Industrial Revolution of 18th century led to the unprecedented growth of industries. Industrialization is associated with the factory system of production.

The family has lost its economic importance. The factories have brought down the prices of commodities, improved their quality and maximized their output. The whole process of production is mechanized. Consequently the traditional skills have declined and good number of artisans has lost their work. Huge factories could provide employment opportunities to thousands of people. Hence men have become workers in a very large number. The process of industrialization has affected the nature, character and the growth of economy. It has contributed to the growth of cities or to the process of urbanization.

Unemployment

The problem of unemployment is a concomitant feature of the rapid technological advancement. Machines not only provide employment opportunities for men but they also take away the jobs of men through labor- saving devices. This results in technological unemployment.

Urbanization

In many countries the growth of industries has contributed to the growth of cities. Urbanization denotes a diffusion of the influence of urban centers to a rural hinterland. Urbanization can be described as a process of becoming urban moving to cities changing from agriculture to other pursuits common to cities and corresponding change of behaviour patterns. Hence only when a large proportion of inhabitants in an area come to cities urbanization is said to occur. Urbanization has become a world phenomenon today. An unprecedented growth has taken place not only in the number of great cities but also in their size. As a result of industrialization people have started moving towards the industrial areas in search of employment. Due to this the industrial areas developed into towns and cities.

Modernization

Modernization is a process which indicates the adoption of the modern ways of life and values. It refers to an attempt on the part of the people particularly those who are custom-bound to adapt themselves to the present-time, conditions, needs, styles and ways in general. It indicates a change in people's food habits, dress habits, speaking styles, tastes, choices, preferences, ideas, values, recreational activities and so on. People in the process of getting themselves modernized give more importance to science and technology. The scientific and technological inventions have modernized societies in various countries. They have brought about remarkable changes in the whole system of social relationship and installed new ideologies in the place of traditional ones.

Development of transport and communication has led to the national and international trade on a large scale. The road transport, the train service, the ships and the aero planes have eased the movement of men and material goods. Post and telegraph, radio and television, newspapers and magazines, telephone and wireless and the like have developed a great deal. The space research and the launching of the satellites for communication purposes have further added to these developments. They have helped the people belonging to different corners of the nation or the world to have regular contacts.

The introduction of the factory system of production has turned the agricultural economy into industrial economy. The industrial or the capitalist economy has divided the social organization into two predominant classes-the capitalist class and the working class. These two classes are always at conflict due to mutually opposite interest. In the course of time an intermediary class called the middle class has evolved.

Technology and War

The dangerous effect of technology is evident through the modern mode of warfare. The weaponry has brought fears and anxieties to the mankind. They can easily destroy the entire human race reveal how technology could be misused. Thus greater the technological advancement the more risk for the mankind.

Changes in Social Institutions

Technology has profoundly altered our modes of life. Technology has not spared the social institutions of its effects. The institutions of family, religion, morality, marriage, state, property have been altered. Modern technology in taking away industry from the household has radically changed the family organization. Many functions of the family have been taken away by other agencies. Marriage is losing its sanctity. It is treated as a civil contract than a sacred bond. Marriages a re becoming more and more unstable. Instances of divorce, desertion and separation are increasing. Technology has elevated the status of women but it has also contributed to the stresses and strains in the relations between men and women at home. Religion is losing hold over the members. People are becoming more secular, rational and scientific but less religious in their outlook. Inventions and discoveries in science have shaken the foundations of religion. The function of the state or the field of state activity has been widened. Modern technology have made the states to perform such functions as -the protection of the aged, the weaker section and the minorities making provision for education, health care etc.Transportation and communication inventions are leading to a shift of functions from local government to the central government of the whole state. The modern inventions have also strengthened nationalism. The modern governments which rule through the bureaucracy have further impersonalized the human relations.

Cultural Lag

To provide a law of social change comparable to the laws of physics and biology that William F. Ogburn in 1922 advanced his theory of social lag.Ogburn pointed out that social changes always originate in the invention by some individual of a new way of doing something new to do. So far he was following in the tradition established by Gabriel Tarde; but Ogburn then began to wander in the tracks of Marx, Historically, he argued, inventions occur most often in the field of material technology, if only because the advantages of an improvement in technology are self-evident. With each development in technology there comes, however, some disturbance to the effective working of the existing social order. A strain or stress is set up between the new technique and various organizational aspects of the social system, changes in which come slowly if at all; the result, disequilibrium between new technology and old social organization, is social lag. The core of Ogburn's theory is the idea that change first occurs in the material technology.

TRANSFORMATIVE SOCIAL CHANGE

Transformative Social Change is a philosophical, practical and strategic process to effect revolutionary change within society, i.e., social transformation. It is effectively a systems approach applied to broad-based social change and social justice efforts to catalyze sociocultural, socioeconomic and political revolution. In seeking to integrate and then politicize personal development and social development as an over-arching approach to social change at multiple levels, addressing a wide range of issues, using holistic, nonviolent methods, it may be best classified as a new social movement. Rather than focus on particular issue(s), it seeks to impact the culture of left of center social movement and organizing work. However, by considering the dismantling of and liberation from oppressive systems, including economic, as core to its goal, it defies even definitions put forth for new social movements. As a comprehensive approach to progressive social change, it seeks distinguishes to itself from the "ordinary" change of conventional social change, social justice and their respective organizing practices by placing emphasis on personal, organizational and social systemic change that cannot be undone, or "deep change."

Components

A key premise defining Transformative Social Change is that "the ends of justice can never be served by the means of injustice, even when the injustice is as subtle as the mental framework instilled by the quest for liberation.("Change vs. Transformation" by Angel Kyodo Williams) Williams further proposes that "because suffering cannot be alleviated by instigating suffering"; the conditions under which social justice activists and seekers operate within organizationally need to exemplify the conditions they wish to ultimately see cultivated within society at large. This ideal coincides with the quote often attributed to Gandhi, "You must be the change you wish to see in the world."

Seeking to better define and cohere the emerging and evolving work of transformative social change, a People's Movement Assembly process was held at the 2010 US Social Forum in Detroit, MI in which the following framework for defining transformation was agreed to by way of resolution:

- Transformation, as applied to social change, is a process through which who we are – individually or collectively – is changed so deeply that the following are altered:
  - (a) identity (way of seeing/thinking/reflecting upon ourselves and environment),
  - (b) emotions (range of feelings and reactivity,)
  - (c) embodiment (relationship and connectedness to and within our bodies and how we show up,)
  - (d) actions (behaviors, patterned responses,)
  - (e) creativity (capacity for responsiveness and ability to access resources,) and
  - (f) paradigms (overall perspective and mode of operating.)

Further, the work of transformation requires the following components:

(a) Awareness of the default conditioning, habits and reactions in our individual, organizational and movement experience.

(b) Appreciation of old identities and states as they pass away and an understanding of the experience of crisis, breakdown, "undone-ness," or "not-knowing" as a necessary catalyst that moves us toward new identities and states. People and entities can and must be supported in these periods.

(c) A container at the individual, organizational

and movement levels; practices that support the process, and a commitment to mentoring people into the necessary skills and processes.

(d) A sustainable relationship with the whole web of life.

- Transformation can and does consist of multi-disciplinary practices, modalities and paths, but overall it points toward the centrality of consistent, rigorous practice capable of undoing conditioning. Such a practice must effect systemic changes, internal and external. We refer to the broad spectrum of varied modalities as transformative practices.
- Transformation happens in its own time, and it can't be undone. We expect processes of transformation, as distinct from change, to be inclined towards being irreversible.
- In the transformation process, one identity or self passes away and a new, radically altered one emerges. The new way of being is more integrated, resourceful and aligned. This is apparent to others in your presence, your actions and your increased capacity to respond based on vision, rather than reaction. This process repeats itself and deepens through continued engagement in transformative practices and processes. The old, previous "form" sheds again and new emerges again.
- The methods and philosophy of transformation must be rooted in an explicit analysis of oppression.
- We recognize that this work is grounded in ancient wisdom, lineages and history, and that it is entering

a new phase of coherence that allows us to move forward.

Basically, applied transformation leads to the following outcomes:

- Radically increased awareness, clarity and comfort with direct experience what is so.
- Breakthroughs in ways of knowing, thinking and accessing creativity
- Impacts our character in a way that is observable, felt and experienced by others.
- Increased ability to respond from a place of vision and compassion rather than ego or self-interest.
- Increased capacity for, skillfulness with and practice of: presence, authenticity and interdependence.

Grants and Awards

In 2009, the Seasons Fund for Social Transformation, a funding collaborative of representatives from small to large foundations, including W. W. Kellogg Foundation, Ford Foundation, Hidden Leaf Fund, Fetzer Institute, Jewish Funds for Justice, Seeds of Justice, Unitarian Universalist Veatch Program and small family funds held an inaugural Transformative Leadership Awards and awarded six collaborative teams $30,000 and two finalists $5,000 for their work in the field.

Transformative Social Change is influenced by the work of social movements led by individuals that are viewed as attending to both their personal/spiritual development as well as systemic social issues because of the "realization that action is not enough":

- Aung San Suu Kyi
- Mohandas Karamchand Gandhi
- Martin Luther King, Jr.
- Black Elk.

In 2002, scholars Raymond Allen Morrow and Carlos Alberto Torres used the phrase "transformative social change" as part of the subtitle in their book *Reading Freire and Habermas: Critical Pedagogy and Transformative Social Change*, Teachers College Press, (ISBN 0-8077-4202-3), 2002 as a term to convey the intersection between Paulo Freire's critical pedagogy and Jürgen Habermas' critical social theory, and the implications those convergences have for educational practice. However, the term is never specifically defined in the book, nor is any distinct theory set forth.

More recently the phrase is being applied as a social change field and movement in which developing inner awareness and nurturing one's inner life, i.e., personal development, is seen as essential in effective social justice work. This is taken to mean from an aligned, sustainable, and nonviolent place. It seeks to operationalize, in practical terms, the ideal of embodiment of the future desired state, in other words, to actualize Gandhi's exhortation to "be the change."

While transformative social change has evolved to include secular practices with no specific spiritual ties, its emphasis on collective liberation shares history, principles and proponents with spiritual activism and liberation spirituality. Likewise, it shares principles of transformative learning and transformative justice, Examples of "transformative practice" include: yoga, meditation, centering prayer, tai chi, forward stance and types of somatic practices.

REFERENCES

"Defining Transformation for Social Change", 2010 US Social Forum People's Movement Assembly, Detroit, MI -June 22–26, 2010.

Horwitz, Claudia and Maceo Vega-Frey, Jesse, "Spiritual Activism & Liberation Spirituality," http://www.stonecircles.org, May 2006.

"Mohandas Karamchand Gandhi" Wikiquote.

Reading Freire and Habermas: Critical Pedagogy and Transformative Social Change, Teachers College Press, 2002.

"Spiritual Activism and Liberation Spirituality: Pathways To Collective Liberation" by Claudia Horwitz & Jesse Maceo Vega-Frey, 2006.

Williams, angel Kyodo; Gass, Robert; Horwitz, Claudia; Vega-Frey, Jesse; Maina, Ng'ethe; Haines, Staci K.; Movement Strategy Center (2010). *Framing Deep Change: Essays on Transformative Social Change*. Third Way Press. pp. 4.

Zimmerman, K., Pathikonda, N., Salgado, B., James, T. (2010). Out of the Spiritual Closet: Organizers Transforming the Practice of Social Justice. Oakland, CA: Movement Strategy Center.

5

Social Action and Social Control

"No action shall be called a social action unless it has relationship with the present, past or future behaviour of others. Others are not necessarily known persons. They may be unknown individuals as well. Social action includes both failures to act and possess acquiescence may be oriented to the past, present or accepted further behaviour of others."

—*Weber*

Max Weber defines social action: action is social in so far as by virtue of the subjective meaning attached to it by acting individual it takes account of the behaviour of others and is thereby oriented in its course. It includes all human behaviour when and in so far as the acting individual attaches a subjective meaning to it.

Pareto is of the opinion that sociology tries to study the logical and illogical aspects of actions. Every social action has two aspects one is its reality and other is its form. Reality involves the actual existence of the thing and the form is the way the phenomenon presents itself to the human mind. The first is called the objective and the other is called subjective aspects.

According to Talcott Parsons a social action is a process in the actor-situation system which has motivational significance to the individual actor or in the case of collectivity, its component individuals.

Different Theories

Sociology according to Weber is not confined to study of social action alone. It studies certain other factors as well. But the basic fact is that social action which according to Max Weber is that action is social in so far as by virtue of the subjective meaning attached to it by acting individual it takes account of the behaviour of others and is thereby oriented in its course.

In fact, social action is not isolated. Social action in order to be really social has to be oriented to the behaviour of other animate things as well. Worship before an idol or worship in a lonely place is not a social action. It has to be oriented to the behaviour of animate beings as well. In every kind of action even overt action is social in the sense of the present discussions. Overt action is non social if it is oriented solely to the behaviour of the inanimate objects.

Result of cooperation and struggle between individual and members of the society: Mere contact with human beings is not a social action. It should deal with the cooperation and struggle between various individuals. A crowd that may collect at a place does not necessarily indulge in the social action unless it starts behaving with one another. Social action is not identical with the similar action, actions of many persons or action influenced by others.

Meaningful understanding with other, action or action of others: Mere contact with others or actions in relation to others are not a social action. Social action should have a meaningful understanding with the social action of others. In every type of contact of human beings has a social character. This is rather confined to cases where the actor's behaviour is meaningfully oriented to that of others.

It is pertinent to note that Weber argued that to explain an action we must interpret it in terms of it's subjectively intended meaning. A person's action is to be explained in terms of the consequences he or she intended purpose rather than in terms of its actual effects the two are often at variance. A subjectively intended meaning is also a causal explanation of the action, in that the end in view is a cause of present actions. For Weber it is important that action is defined in terms of meaningfulness and sociological analysis must proceed by identifying the meaning that actions have for actors.

Main Types

In the opinion of Max Weber social action like other social forms of action may be classified in the following four types:

1. *Rational Action:* In terms of rational orientation to a system of discrete individual ends that is through expectations as to the behaviour of objects in the external situation and of other human individuals making use of these expectations as conditions or means for the successful attainment of the actor's own rationally chosen ends.
2. *Evaluative actions:* In terms of rational orientation to an absolute valuc; involving a conscious belief in the absolute value of some ethical, aesthetic, religious or other form of behaviour entirely for its own sake and independently of any prospects of external success.
3. *Emotional actions:* In terms of effectual orientation especially emotional determined by

the specific affects and state of feeling of the actors.

4. *Traditional actions:* Traditionally oriented through the habituation of long practice.

In fact, sociology according to Weber is not merely confined to study of social action. It is an interpretative understanding of the social action. He has defined sociology as a science of understanding. Although he has laid stress on causal explanation and causal relationship or relationship between cause and effect but he clearly defines the difference between the two. He has not only differentiated between sociology and natural sciences but sociology and other social sciences as well.

Talcott Parson's theory of social action is based on his concept of the society. Parsons is known in the field of sociology mostly for his theory of social action. Action is a process in the actor-situation system which has motivational significance to the individual actor or in the case of collectively, its component individuals. On the basis of this definition it may be said that the processes of action are related to and influenced by the attainment of the gratification or the avoidance of deprivations of the correlative actor, whatever they concretely be in the light of the relative personal structures that there may be.

All social actions proceed from mechanism which is their ultimate source. It does not mean that these actions are solely connected with organism. They are also connected with actor's relations with other persons' social situations and culture.

Various Systems

Generally, social actions are guided by the following

three systems which may also be called as three aspects of the systems of social action:

1. *Personality system:* This aspect of the system of social action is responsible for the needs for fulfilment of which the man makes effort and performs certain actions. But once man makes efforts he has to meet certain conditions. These situations have definite meaning and they are distinguished by various symbols and symptoms. Various elements of the situation come to have several meanings for ego as signs or symbols which become relevant to the organization of his expectation system.
2. *Cultural system:* Once the process of the social action develops the symbols and the signs acquire general meaning. They also develop as a result of systematised system and ultimately when different actors under a particular cultural system perform various social interactions, special situation develops.
3. *Social System:* A social system consists in a plurity of individual actor's interacting with each other in a situation which has at least a physical or environmental aspect actors are motivated in terms of tendency to the optimization of gratification and whose relations to the situation including each other is defined and motivated in terms of system of culturally structured and shaped symbols.

Remarkably, in Parson's view each of the three main type of social action systems—culture, personality and social systems has a distinctive coordinative role in the action process and therefore has some degree of causal autonomy.

Thus personalities organize the total set of learned needs, demands and action choices of individual actors, no two of whom are alike.

It is pertinent to note that every social system is confronted with four functional problems. These problems are those of pattern maintenance, integration, goal attainment and adaptation. Pattern maintenance refers to the need to maintain and reinforce the basic values of the social system and to resolve tensions that emerge from continuous commitment to these values. Integration refers to the allocation of rights and obligations, rewards and facilities to ensure the harmony of relations between members of the social system. Goal attainment involves the necessity of mobilizing actors and resources in organized ways for the attainment of specific goals. Adaptation refers to the need for the production or acquisition of generalized facilities or resources that can be employed in the attainment of various specific goals.

Social systems tend to differentiate these problems so as to increase the functional capabilities of the system. Such differentiation whether through the temporal specialization of a structurally undifferentiated unit or through the emergence of two or more structurally distinct units from one undifferentiated unit is held to constitute a major verification of the fourfold functionalist schema.

It also provides the framework within which are examined the plural interchanges that occur between structurally differentiated units to provide them with the inputs they require in the performance of their functions and to enable them to dispose of the outputs they produce.

Pattern Variables

Self-orientation vs collectivity orientation: This dichotomy depends on social norms or shared expectations which define as legitimate the pursuit of the actor's private interests or obligate him to act in the interests of the group.

Affectivity vs affectivity neutrality: The pattern is affective when an organized action system emphasizes gratification that is when an actor tries to avoid pain and to maximize pleasure; the pattern is affectively neutral when it imposes discipline and renouncement or deferment of some gratifications in favour of other interests.

Particularism vs universalism: The former refers to standards determined by an actor's particular relations with particular relations with a particular object; the latter refers to value standards that are highly generalized.

Diffusion vs specificity: This is the dilemma of defining the relations borne by object to actor as indefinitely wide in scope, infinitely broad in involvement morally obligating and significant in pluralistic situations or specifically limited in scope and involvement.

Quality vs performance: The choice between modalities of the social object. This is the dilemma of according primary treatment to an object on the basis of what it is in itself an inborn quality or what it does and quality of its performance. The former involves defining people on the basis of certain attributes such as age, sex, color, nationality etc; the latter defines people on the basis of their abilities.

Karl Mannheim's theory of sociology of knowledge explains the linkage between thought and action. Thought process is not of individual making. Rather a group having similar position develop only gradually new thoughts as differentiated from the old established thoughts when they are exposed to a certain kind of typical behaviour in a prolonged historical setting and social perspective. When the actors interact in certain social reality they organize their thought and act in a historical and social perspective.

Similarly, Pareto has discussed his action theory on the basis of logical and illogical actions in which both objective and subjective meanings are attached respectively.

Logical action essentially involves rational action both in the mind of the actor as well as those who observe them objectively. He maintains a logical co-relation between the means to the action and the end it serves. All sorts of logical actions are objectively observable and verifiable which is a reality in itself.

However in social reality most of the social actions are not logical. Although sociology deals with both the logical and non-logical actions it emphasizes the analysis of non-logical actions. It is the social reality in which actors give subjective meaning to the action which is driven by meanings, motives and sentiments.

After having a clear understanding of social action and its role in social mobilization social movement now we come to the issue of social control.

SOCIAL CONTROL

> "Social control is an influence where influence may be exerted through public opinion, coer-cion, social suggestion, religion or any other method. The influence is exerted by the society which means that group is better able to exercise in-fluence over the individual than a single individual. This group may be the family, the church, the state or the trade union etc.The effectiveness of the influence however depends on variable factors. Sometimes family may exercise more effective influence than the state or vice-versa."

MacIver defines social control as the way in which entire social order coheres and maintains itself –how it operates itself as a whole as a changing equilibrium. Mannheim defines social control as the sum of those methods by which a society tries to influence human behavior to maintain a given order.

To Ogbuand an established rule is social control. Ogburn and Nimkoff the patterns of pressure which a society exerts to maintain order E Ross defines it the system of devices whereby society brings its members into conformity with the accepted standards of behavior.

According to Lapiere social control is a corrective for inadequate socialization. G.A Lundberg has defined social control as designating those social behaviors which influence individuals or groups towards conformity to established or desired norms.

In the words of Kimball Young social control is the use of coercion, force, restraint, suggestion or persuasion of one group over another or of a group over its members or of persons over others to enforce the prescribed rules of the game. These rules may be set down by the members themselves as in a professional code of ethics or they may be those laid down by a larger, more inclusive group for the regulation of other smaller groups.

The influence is exercised for promoting the welfare of the group as a whole. The person is influenced to act in the interest of others rather than in accordance with his own individual interests. Social control is exercised for some specific end in view. The aim is always the wel-fare of the whole. The individual is made conscious of other's existence; their interests. He is made to adhere to the appropriate social ways.

Social Control and Socialization

It is pertinent to note that social control and socialization are closely related to each other. Social control is a part of socialization. During the process of socialization the process of social control also is in op-eration. Through socialization social control becomes effective. In order to maintain the so-cial order there are definite procedures in society. These customs and procedures become a part of man's life and man gets adjusted to the society. As a matter of fact, societies depend heavily upon effective socialization to internalize social norms and values as the individual's guides and motives to action. Through socialization societies aim to control the behavior of its members subconsciously. The various agencies of socialization like family, state, school, club etc are also the agencies of social control. They exercise regulatory influence over the behavior of the individual.

Why Social Control?

Social solidarity is essential for the existence of society.No two persons is alike in their na-ture, ideas, attitudes and interests. Every individual is a separate personality. There are cul-tural differences among the individuals. As a matter of fact society is a heterogeneous or-ganization. If every individual is allowed unrestricted freedom to act and behave, it may cre-ate social disorder. For an orderly social life social control is necessary.

The aims of social control are to bring out conformity, solidarity and continuity of a particular group or society. Social control is necessary for maintaining order in the society. It is necessary for every soci-ety or group to maintain its social order and this is possible only when its members behave in accordance with that social order. An important objective of social control is to maintain the old order.

Although enforcement of the old order in a changing society may hinder so-cial progress, yet it is necessary to maintain continuity and uniformity in society. Without social control social unity would be a mere dream. Social control regulates behavior in accordance with established norms which brings uniformity of behavior and leads to unity among the individuals.

The family maintains its unity because its members behave in a simi-lar manner in accordance with family norms. No two men are alike in their attitudes, ideas, interests and habits. Even the children of same parents do not have the same attitudes, habits or interests. Men believe in different religions, dress, eat differently and have different ideologies.

There are so many differences in the ways of living of the people that at every moment there is the possibility of clash be-tween them. In modern times this possibility has all the more increased because man has become too self-centred.Social control is necessary to protect social interests and satisfy common needs. If social control is removed and every individual is left to behave freely so-ciety would be reduced to a state of lawlessness. Social control provides social sanction to the social ways of behavior. There are numerous folkways, modes and customs prevalent in society. Every individual has to follow them. If an individual violates the social norm; he is compelled through social control to observe them. Thus social control provides sanction to social norms.

In fact, the study of social control is an important aspect of sociology. It is a significant field of study. It is a unifying factor in the study of human behavior. According to Kimball Young the aims of social control are to bring about conformity, solidarity and continuity of particular group or society. These aims are good but most individuals who endeavor to control their fellow men show little perspective in their efforts.

They want that others should accept the modes of conduct which they themselves prefer. This preference may be based on any fac-tor-experience derived in life, desire to exploit others for one's own gain, political, personal or economic. Some reformers and leaders try to conceal their motives by good reasons in the form of al-truistic rationalization. A newspaper advertisement that offer discount to those who make purchases by a particular date is an example of such rationalizations. It is difficult to know and classify the motives of the agents of social control.

Purpose

1. Exploitative, motivated by self interest.
2. Regulative based upon habit and the desire for behavior of the customary types
3. Creative or constructive based on social benefit

In fact, results of social control are not always beneficial to society or to the individual. Even social control for constructive purposes may confuse the public and end in inactivity. Efforts to regulate behavior in accordance to custom may cause cultural lag, mental conflict and emotional instability.

How to Control?

The means by which individuals are induced or compelled to conform to the usages and life values of the group are so numerous and varied that a classification is not possible.E.A Ross has described a number of means that have been used by social groups throughout the human history to keep individuals under control. The important among them are public opin-ion, law, custom, religion, morality, personality, folkways and mores.

E.C Hayes distinguished between control by sanctions and control by suggestion and imita-tion. According to him, education is the most effective means of control and the family is the most significant agency. Karl Mannheim distinguished between direct means of social control and indirect means of social control. Luther L Bernard distinguished between unconscious and conscious means of control.The most important among the unconscious means of control are custom, tradition and convention.

The conscious means of control are those which have been consciously developed and employed by leaders of all types. According to him conscious means of control are more ef-fective than unconscious ones though the influence of the latter also is quite marked. He also talked about exploitative and constructive methods of social control. Exploitative means are such as punishment, reprisals, intimidation, censorship and repression.

Among the constructive means are included revolution, custom, law, education and social reform, on-violent coercion and belief in supernatural forces. Some sociologists have classified the social control into informal and formal means.Sympathy, sociability, resentment, the sense of justice, public opinion, folkways and mores are some of the informal means of social control. They are very powerful in primary social groups where interaction is on a personal basis.

The effectiveness of the informal means of control though somewhat lessened in modern large communities wherein con-tacts tend to be impersonal may still be observed in small villages. In modern times the in-formal methods have given place to formal ones such as laws, education, coercion and codes.

Law: It is pertinent to note that law is the most important formal means of social control. Early societies depended upon informal means of social control but when societies grew in size and complexity they were compelled to formulate rules and regulations which define the required types of behavior and specify the penalties to be imposed upon those who violate them. Law is a body of rules enacted by legally authorized bodies and enforced by authorized agencies.

It defines clearly rights, duties as well as the punishments for their violation. The modern societies are large in size. Their structure is complex consisting of a number of groups, organizations, institutions and vested interests. Informal means of social control are no longer sufficient to maintain social order and harmony.

Remarkably, in modern society relationships are of secondary nature. Security of life and property as well as the systematic ordering of relationships make formalization of rules necessary. Law pre-scribes uniform norms and penalties throughout a social system.What were in mores and customs earlier has now been formalized into a body of law.

Law prohibits certain actions for example anti-touchability act prohibits untouchability in any form and a person practis-ing untouchability is liable to punishment. Prohibition act forbids drinking at public places. In this way law exercises a powerful influence upon the behavior of people in modern socie-ties.

Coercion: Coercion is the use of force to achieve a desired end. It may be physical or non-violent. It is the ultimate means of social control when all other means fail. Physical coercion may take the form of bodily injury, imprisonment and death penalty. Physical coercion is without doubt the lowest form of social control. Societies would least desire to use it. If a society has to depend on external force it shows its weakness rather than strength in social control.

Further, Nonviolent coercion consists of strike; boycott and non-cooperation.the students may go on strike to ensure better hostel facilities. Boycott is the withholding of social or economic in-teraction with others to express disapproval and to force acceptance of demands.Non co-operation is refusal to cooperate. The teachers may refuse to cooperate with the manage-ment over the payment of salaries.Non-violent coercion can be a successful way of effecting social control.

The importance of education as a means of social control is being increasingly realized. Edu-cation is a process of socialization. It prepares the child for social living. It reforms the atti-tudes wrongly formed by the children. Thus a family may make the child superstitious; edu-cation will correct his beliefs and remove his prejudices. It teaches him value of discipline, social cooperation, tolerance and sacrifice. It instills in him the qualities of honesty, air play and a sense of right and wrong. The importance of education for creating right social atti-tudes among youth cannot be overlooked.

6

Reconceptualising Social Movement

Here in this chapter we will present a reconceptualisation of social movements having a case study of Swayam Sikshan Prayog (SSP) as basis.

It is pertinent to mention first that social movement theories and concepts typically have been analysed using the individual member of an organisation (Olson 1971) or the social movement organisation (SMO) as the unit of analysis (Zald and McCarthy 1987). Neither unit captures the totality of what constitutes a movement.

Typically, a movement is a result of a concerted effort on the part of several individuals, organisations, and networks. Only recently have studies emerged on the functioning of networks of organisations (Knoke 1990).

Even here, intermediate levels of organisation which exist between the organisation and the individual, such as the collective, have not been analysed; nor have the forms of movement organisations been explicitly linked to the material conditions of their participants from a class and gender perspective.

Taking in view the case of the Swayam Shikshan Prayog (SSP) any theoretical analysis has to take into account the fact that the movement participants are women and has to occur at four levels: the individual woman's level; the collective level; the organisational level; and at the level of the network. Only through the use of such an analytical framework can we examine the complexity of organisational forms and the various facets of organisational characteristics, such as formal organisation, decentralisation, size, and the types of issues addressed by SMOs. This analytical format, with a distinct gender analysis, frames the discussion that follows on the formation and evolution of movements and the use of relevant concepts developed by social movement theory.

Causes

Most classical theories of social movements, to which the Collective Behaviour school belongs, attribute the rise of movements to structural strain, social isolation, changing expectations, or some combination of the above. The commonality of grievances is stressed by the collective behaviour approach (Smelser 1963) and recognised by other schools as a necessary, but not sufficient condition for a movement to take place. However, the Resource Mobilisation school posits that movement participants only participate in a movement if they have a material incentive to do so.

Gendering of Grievances: While we retain the validity of the concept that movement participants need a common set of grievances to come together and to participate in a movement, it needs to be modified in the case of grassroots women. Grievances are gendered to the extent that women and men share some common concerns but women bring to the table an additional set of concerns.

Women's primary responsibility for reproduction and

towards the nurturing and sustenance of their families manifest in these community-based struggles as a collective demand for improved living conditions including better nutrition, better education for their children, better government services to their communities, increased availability of clean water, fuel, fodder, or what are termed 'consumption related necessities. These demands are interwoven with demands for credit and assets to improve their productive capacities as economic actors.

In fact, women become more active, often as a prequisite to their participation, gender relations within communities are also challenged in this wide gamut of issues. All development issues are women's issues, which are interrelated. Therefore when an organisation or collective begins to organise around one set of issues (for instance, work, alcoholism, or deforestation), their concerns soon broaden to include other issues as well.

Addressing a wide range of questions was one factor that helped the movement sustain itself and renew the interest of its constituents, since through the learning exchanges ((*shibirs, melas* visits to other groups, study tours) each collective would learn about and adopt new issues addressed by others in the net-work. The result was the constant adoption of new issues and a constant learning, across collectives, of new strategies to tackle old problems.

These grievances varied not just because of the involvement of women but because at different organisational levels—the collective, the organisation, and the network—the concerns changed. Broadly speaking, women in the SSP shared in common the myriad issues related to poverty and survival. The collectives, the organisations, and the network, while they maintained this central focus, also had concerns larger than those of individual women.

Commonality of Grievances

Women: The main concern voiced by women was their lack of incomes, information, and access to material resources. In real terms, these concerns translated into the need for better living conditions, for jobs, incomes, credit, land, and assets. Most women lived with their families either working a small field or doing seasonal agricultural wage labour. Often, this meant that for six months out of the year they earned no wages. When asked what would help alleviate poverty, a common response from women was 'A business'.

When organisations were unable to address these very basic concerns, women's participation in organisational activities started to wane.

Women's Collectives: While each collective represented the collective demands of women, i.e., their own survival and that of their families, it also had larger concerns, which included providing an alternative voice to village-level development decisions that affected entire communities, involving as many poor women as possible and fostering a sustainable form of development more conducive to their survival and that of their families. Sometimes, the collective's concerns would clash with those of individual women, as its aim was the inclusion of the largest number possible and the expansion of its membership. This meant sharing the collective's resources and a shift in the collective's goal away from benefiting the individual woman to benefiting all poor women in that village.

It meant that once poor women were helped financially or gained new insights information or were assisted in some way by the collective, they had a responsibility to share this opportunity with other women and not monopolise the benefits gained from the collective.

Interviews conducted with women's groups pointed to several examples where the objectives of the collective were inconsistent with those of individual women. One concrete instance of this clash was in cases where the collective consisted of women belonging to different castes. In these instances, upper-caste members of a women's group would be required to eat with and mingle freely among women from other castes in larger meetings. Here the concerns of each individual upper-caste/lower-caste woman would be weighed against the collective's overall goal of treating all women equally.

Another example is that of the collective turning down requests for money made under family pressure by individual women for their husbands or other male members in their families. Usually, other women in a collective knew whether a woman was requesting money for herself or for others, because strong community networks and ties between women afforded them that familiarity. Broadly speaking, the collective's concerns reflected not only those of individual women, but also the common concerns of all poor women in the community and the problems faced by the village community at large.

Organisations: A sense of declining legitimacy, stemming from feelings of ineffectiveness due to the inability of organisations to address the economic needs of women, had forced organisers to begin a collective exploration of potential economic resources available to women via the network. This exploration brought up conflicting issues pertaining to external control and autonomy of the organisation, including not only control by the government and other funding agencies, but also by other organisations within the network. Equally important for organisations was their concern to maintain the autonomy of the women's groups.

This was largely, though not always, based on an accompanying ideological belief that the mass base (poor women in this case) should have minimal contact with the government. In other words, even where organisations received government funds, such as the PFC, according to one organiser, 'the mass base should not be corrupted by any contact with government; people should be protected from the bureaucracy".

In fact, the women themselves did not view the acceptance of government funds as problematic since their survival was contingent on their increased access to resources. A loss of some autonomy for women weighed against the option for survival often resulted in women choosing the latter. Most organisations, on the other hand, would have backed out if more resources meant a threat to their autonomy. Yet, if the network had been unable to mobilise resources for the local work of organisations, many would have lost interest.

In fact one organiser, Leela More said that, 'till government collaboration began and the funding possibilities increased, the SSP was not so important to my work'. Hence, the sustained participation of organisations in the SSP was contingent on the network's capacity to mobilise resources, not solely for the network's activities, but to support organisations' local activities and to provide these resources without any threat to their autonomy.

Organisations were also simultaneously exploring funding avenues outside the government, such as foreign funding agencies. The network had to cater to needs at all levels—the mass base, women's groups, and organisations. While these negotiations were rooted in expanding the opportunities available to poor women to improve their living and working conditions, they were also based on other considerations which included preserving the decentralised, informal, voluntary nature of participation by the organisations and the collectives.

Besides this, the resources generated had to be flexible enough so that each individual collective could utilise them, given its current structure and its lack of formal organisation, such that the poorest among women could obtain them. If the grievances varied at each level of the SSP, did the incentive structures also change?

Incentives

Individual Women: The primary incentive for the individual woman to participate in this movement was the possibility of increasing the chances of survival for herself and her family. Through the collective, women could get loans and participate in income-generating projects together. Mainly, the potential to get credit from informal savings groups formed by women, organisational funds, state subsidies, and bank loans formed the bulk of material incentives. Because poor women have very few options to earn money, both the government and NGOs in India are more easily able to organise them into collectives.

Similarly, other incentives included the myriad opportunities for learning through their participation in the collective. Women gained confidence in dealing with the public' world, which is reflected in all aspects of their lives.

The 'collective' represents an alternative learning space for women and is the only 'school' that women can attend.

It is through the collective alone that women learn skills such as handling money, negotiating with authorities, and so forth.

Women's Collectives: The incentive structures for women's collectives should be examined in terms of access to organisational and public resources. Prior to the collaboration with the state, only organisational funds and funds generated through savings and credit groups were available to women's collectives. Through the pilot project and the state's involvement, funds were available in far greater quantities in the form of non-competitive public goods, which could be demanded as a right by the collectives directly from the state.

In fact, the clearest incentive structures existed more for the collective than for the individual woman or the organisation, because the resources available via DWCRA were released only to collectives. It was the collective that would own any assets obtained through DWCRA, not the individual woman, or the organisation. However, this did not prevent the individual woman from earning an income or getting credit through her participation in the collective and through the collective's participation in the pi-lot project.

If an individual woman wanted to do a project which the collective had not agreed upon, she had to rely on the credit pools of the collective, organisational funds, or on other government programmes (such as the IRDP) which specifically serviced individuals. The means through which women increased their bargaining skills, communication skills, capacity to handle money, and so forth were also primarily through their involvement in the group.

Organisations: The material incentives for each organisation to join the network's activities were more resources that would be available for its local work with existing women's groups, for the expansion of its work and of its membership base through the formation of new women's groups, and for organisational activities such as 'training and exchanges. Other incentives included increasing the visibility and bargaining power of the organisations vis-a-vis state and other elites. Each organisation could potentially lobby for and obtain the same amount of resources for the women's groups they worked with, from their district government agencies.

Organisations such as ASSEFA hired more women, while smaller organisations such as SJVS trained the women in existing collectives *to* organise new collectives and thus expand their out-each to new villages. Still others were just beginning to work with women's groups for the first time due to the increased availability of resources and their interaction with the network.

The pilot project with the state therefore resulted in restructuring organisational staff and reshaping organisational goals to be more inclusive of women. The incentive for small organisations to join was higher than for the larger organisations, as these were also the organisations with the least amount of resources that had in the past been unable to address the economic concerns of poor women and were becoming increasingly concerned about their legitimacy with women. However, even for the larger organisations the possibility of making state resources available to women's groups on terms more palatable to them was one form of incentive.

For both the larger and smaller organisations, however, the material incentives were tempered by the possibilities of government cooption and the potential loss of autonomy within the network itself. Organisations understood the advantages of the exchanges organised through the SSP.

They saw more funds coming in through the network for these exchanges from outside funding agencies. The intensification of exchanges between organisations and women's groups were seen as a direct result of the workshops and events organised through the network. For many organisations, a political learning process ensued on the working of state mechanisms and for the first time many started learning how to interact with the different state agencies and different levels of the bureaucracy. This proved to be an enriching, though difficult, experience. Material incentives are increasingly weighed against other kinds of considerations as one moves from the individual to larger levels of organisation.

While clear material incentives existed for organisations to participate in this collaboration, it was complicated by the need for them to operate through the state. Organisations felt accountable to women and expressed a sense of unease and insecurity of the long-term repercussions of this collaboration with the state, further complicated by the fact that through income generation several women's collectives would be now entering the market economy. Even when women's collectives articulated the desire to get involved with the pilot project, several organisation leaders felt women in isolated villages could not possibly understand the entire repercussions of this involvement.

This was a consequence of ideologies that opposed any direct collaboration with the state or ideologies opposed to income generation or involvement with the market economy. Several organisation leaders felt conflicted about the network's activities with the state and decided to periodically re-evaluate their desire to continue this interaction, deepen it, limit it or withdraw from it entirely.

Organisational leadership also had before them the historical lessons learned from state involvement in the cooperative movement, among others, where these movements were to a large extent coopted by the state. This brings us to the analysis of how the movement grew, what the movement's goals were and how these goals helped shape the form the organisations took in the movement.

Evolution of SSP

The complexity of the considerations raised by the different organisational entities within the movement that had to be weighed against each other which not only resulted in the evolution of a complex form of organisation such as the SSP, but each entity—the network, the organisation and the collective— served very different purposes and assumed different characteristics. The growth of this movement happened in several stages, with the collectives and organisations evolving first and the network emerging later. The collective is a smaller unit than the organisation it is affiliated to and serves a multitude of purposes. Primarily, the collective provided a public space and a time for women in a community to meet and it is in this 'alternative' space where consciousness raising occurs. The collective also served as a voice that articulated the concerns of the community in which it is located and in that sense was the primary decision-making unit at the level of the community. The collective, unlike the organisation, is situated right in the community and this location is crucial to the sustained participation of women, especially given the restrictions on their mobility.

The concerns therefore varied and were prioritised

differently in each community. Tribal women's collectives often began around the issue of fighting alcoholism among men. Collectives in the drought prone areas, on the other hand, were primarily concerned about drinking water, the lack of agricultural employment due to drought conditions, and the like. Another purpose was to allow resources to be adapted locally to the needs, skills, and particular conditions that its members face in their daily lives. Its small size allowed strong personal ties and the development of collective leadership and action. The evolution of the organisation, a larger, formal entity with paid staff and record-keeping capabilities allowed for the movement to interface and transfer resources from the state and other formal institutions to the collectives.

The organisation, at least in the initial stages, facilitates the creation of groups/collectives and subsequently fora for dialogue between women and the state and other formal institutional representatives.

In fact, transfer of resources necessitates the need for formal and informal organisation as well as the processes of interaction. Formal processes involve negotiations between movement actors and the state, banks, or other formal institutions. Informal processes occur for the purposes of the exchange of information between women leaders and activists across collectives and organisations and take the form of *shibirs, melas,* field visits by women leaders and activists to other organisations or women's groups, and so forth. In these informal exchanges often times officials from formal institutions, i.e., the government, banks, and donor agencies, would be invited for the purpose of increasing the exposure of women to these actors in an alternative environment as well as to sensitise officials to women's needs through their exposure to grassroots women.

The movement owes its evolution to the shifting opportunities for women in the SSP as a result of the network's activities and the pilot project. Here, we will employ the concepts of Resource Mobilisation school (RMS) and Political Process School (PPS) to examine the growth of the movement, namely, the changes in the political opportunity structure (POS), the resources mobilised which allowed for expansion of the movement, and the concept of elite involvement.

Resources Mobilisation

Looking at the network's capacity to mobilise resources, one saw a tremendous increase in the resources in circulation after 1988 in the form of events, exchanges, and training activities. This trend was accentuated by the linkages established with the state and banks in 1991. Funding agencies were approached to facilitate exchanges and networking at the local, district, state, and interstate levels.

Ultimately, the reason organisations in the SSP continued working with each other was that the network' activities came as a direct response to the needs articulated by women in local forums. A few organisations continued participating, despite being skeptical, because women in their organisations had expressed the need for work and incomes (through income generation, linkages to state programmes, credit enhancement) in local forums held with women's collectives. Other reasons why they continued to work within the network were the network's informal and loose structure, which did not force organisations to swear allegiance to the network.

Furthermore, government funds could be used in very different ways by different organisations, since DWCRA was flexible in how its funds were utilised.

Using DWCRA as an entry point, resources from other government programmes were also tapped. For instance, organisations working with people located in forest areas were able to use funds from the Department of Horticulture for reforestation programmes or for forest-based production.

Organisations such as SJVS, working on income-generation projects such as tailoring, were able to use DWCRA to fund the production of ready-made garments and simultaneously applied to TRYSEM to train women in tailoring. Similarly, for organisations and collectives interested in watershed development, agricultural production, land-based activities, funds from DWCRA were adapted to fund these activities, while supplementary funds were sought from JRY and other government agencies/programmes. For the organisation, the collective, and the women, the capacity to mobilise resources depended intrinsically on the collective bargaining strength of the network and the resultant change in POS. The discussion on the POS follows.

Political Opportunity Structure

The political process model emphasises the changing structure of opportunities for movement participants. The assumption here is that even when groups are organised, unless there are openings in the POS a movement may not succeed. The opposite is also true, i.e., a movement may not occur even if presented with a favourable structure of political openings without the supportive organisational environment.

The political opportunity structure (POS) is a dynamic concept. It helps draw comparisons between the political opportunities available to: individual women who belong to a collective and to those who do not collectives that are affiliated to an NGO and to those that are affiliated to the state; collectives and organisations that belong to a network and to those that do not. In the SSP case, the POS, therefore, changed over time because women mobilised into collectives and later these collectives and organisations federated into loose networks.

Let us examine the POS afforded to voluntary organisations by poverty alleviation programmes such as DWCRA. Being a national programme, like several other such programmes, resources from DWCRA could potentially be obtained by any voluntary organisation or women's collective in the country. NGOs could either lobby for these resources by themselves if they were large enough, as is the CDF, or through networks such as the SSP.

However, large organisations—CDF, WWF, and SEWA—are the exception. Ninety per cent of organisations in the NGO sector tend to be small; and for these organisations, interacting through networks is the best way they can lobby to take over state programmes. Several networks of NGOs exist all over India. Few networks, however, were able to access resources for the local activities of organisations, either from government, or banks, or other outside sources, like the SSP did.

The question then arises as to why this type of activity was not happening on a larger scale, given the network's potential to obtain funds from a variety of government programmes; that similar incentives exist for organisations, collectives, and women; and that women in these organisations shared a similar set of grievances, (namely, issues around poverty and survival). In other words, assuming that there existed a POS favourable to such activities, why did the SSP represent more the exception than the rule?

This was because the SSP was able to create a nonthreatening environment where NGOs and women's groups could collectively reflect on their experiences and interact with the state on terms which were more conducive to the needs of poor women. It afforded organisations, and women's groups the possibility of interaction without a loss of autonomy. As a result it did not encounter many of the problems that other NGOs typically face in their dealings with the state.

It is pertinent to note that while poverty alleviation programmes existed in all states in India, the degree to which each state government is open to negotiations influences the possibility of collaboration. Non-governmental organisations often do not obtain funds from DWCRA or from any other national programme. Many choose not to, out of the fear that working with the state would increase the state's potential to control the organisation's activities. Second, even those who believe it is possible to work with the state do not have adequate information about government programmes.

Many with knowledge of these programmes are too small and do not have the capacity to bargain with the state. Some others, either because they are too small or are not part of larger networks, find district government agencies uninterested in collaborating with them. When a single organisation tries to collaborate with the government, rarely does it have the clout to change the terms of implementation of state programmes.

The rigid terms of the programmes and the structures of the bureaucracy lend themselves to the rapid breakdown in the relationship with NGOs. This leads to widespread disillusionment and the conclusion that working with the state is a waste of time. Often, advocacy by networks of organisations focus on legislative changes or on influencing public opinion around issues which activated the network's formation in the first place.

Once this crisis was over, usually the network's activities died down and people's participation waned. The SSP, in contrast, was not responding to a short-term crisis but was built first around evolving a shared perspective and experiences around the issue of livelihoods for poor women. It was taking on a long-term restructuring process of social and economic relationships within villages changing state policies and programmes to respond to the Reeds of poor women and creating mechanisms they required.

The creation of structures needed by poor women simultaneously meant the creation of state infrastructure and programmes geared towards them. This included the lobbying for national programmes such as DWCRA. Women's collectives involved in economic production expressed the need for worksheds, storage units, and sales outlets. The SSP, in response, started negotiations with the Department of Rural Development for infrastructure to provide worksheds from another programme, JRY; then began lobbying for storage and sales outlets for women where either existing infrastructure or funds (from DWCRA or JRY) could be used. Multipurpose centres provided by DWCRA could also be used for storage and sales.

SSP-SPARC, as a resource organisation, through its past experience via SPARC with the urban poor, was particularly skilled in conducting negotiations with the state. It was also skilled at obtaining and processing information on potential resources available through both private foundations and the state, and being able to then repackage this information to make it accessible to organisations and women's groups.

These skills and the work of a full-time secretariat which undertook the functions of obtaining information, translating it into vernacular, circulating it, and lobbying at the state level gave the SSP activists an advantage that few other networks possessed.

The SSP was able to prioritise the process of interaction rather than the network's structure in practice. Fundamentally this rested in its capacity to centre and direct its activities towards creating new spaces for women's participation and dialogue with key actors. The choice of a programme like DWCRA, which was flexible in the uses of its funds, was critical in sustaining the participation of organisations and women's collectives. Organisations in the SSP were able to continue working on issues they were involved in prior to the interaction with the network. The difference was that now women's groups were increasingly the focus of their work and more funds were available to support the activities of the groups.

The political opportunity structure is distinct at each level (village, block, district, state) of this organisational form. For each women's group—on paper at least—funds were potentially available wherever the programme was operational. This meant that 2,600 women's groups in about 52 different districts across India could potentially apply to the DWCRA programme. However, in practice, government officials usually decided where the money would be allocated and to whom.

This was often determined by patronage ties defined by caste, class, and education. Sometimes, men would find out about government programmes for women and get their spouses to apply. Sometimes, local elites such as the members of the panchayat or the village-level government, or wives from rich families in the village applied for this money. Information about these programmes was rarely available to poor women.

Organisations often sought information about potential sources of funds. However, interviews revealed that prior to the SSP's activities very few organisers had heard of DWCRA or any other such programmes. Information about government resources is usually available in a technical format, not easily understood by most people, even organisers, whether literate or not. Organiser who in the past had tried to apply to DWCRA in conjunction with women's groups found that very few of the women they organised were actually eligible for this money. Organisational funds would have to supplement a collective of women who did not officially qualify for government funding. Often, organisations were unable to do this and the uneven distribution of funds led to disharmony within the groups.

Usually, the procedure at DWCRA was such that if one woman was found to be ineligible, the proposal for the entire group would get rejected, thus delaying the entire process for as long as a whole year. As it turned cut, applying for any form of government funding was a tedious, often disheartening process. The stories which organisers and women told of their individual attempts in the past to get government funds was one long saga of applications, rejections, re-applications, delays, partial approvals, and so on. There were few, if any, success stories of women getting government funds, with or without the help of organisers.

This finding was corroborated by other writers who found that most national government programmes were inaccesable to poor women due to the centralised and bureaucratic nature of the funding process. Often, an organisation's size determined its ability to get government funds. Larger organisations would sometimes visit government offices and successfully negotiate funds and better conditions of resource availability. However, more often than not, most organisations were too small to bargain for resources.

Hence, the POS was such that these funds were inaccessible to most individual organisations and collectives. Even though the money was present in the district-level budgets, the implementation conditions and eligibility criteria of the programme needed to be changed for the money to be made available to women who really needed it, for which state-wide policy changes were needed. Individual organisations operating within their respective districts did not have the capacity to influence such change. As shown, even for a large organisation conditions did not change, despite the collaboration between the government and the NGO being forged at the state level.

It took a network of organisations like the SSP to change these conditions through systematic policy feedback from districts across Maharashtra.

For the individual woman, DWCRA was inaccessible. She had to be part of a group for it to be available to her. Only in those districts where women's groups existed, could women get these funds. Women who were organised had a fighting chance of obtaining this money relative to women who were not. Even so, as outlined earlier, the chances were slim.

As such, while the DWCRA programme was originally available in 52 districts spread across several states in India, of which only a few were in Maharashtra. The SSP network was able to initiate the DWCRA programme in six new districts in Maharashtra. This, in and of itself, carved out new government budgets and spaces for women in these districts thereby expanding the availability of government resources to about 300 new women's groups per year, an avenge of 6,000 women. The planned expansion of the pilot project to implement DWCRA in 15 districts in Maharashtra would further expand the access to double the existing number of women's groups. This expansion would further allow mere organisations to use DWCRA as a means to organise women's groups.

The strategy of targeting state resources is highly contested among movement actors and theorists alike. In the context of this particular movement, the discussion on the involvement of state elites needs to be contextualised along with the examination of other local elites.

Elite Involvement

According to the Resource Mobilisation school, increased elite involvement is seen as essential to increasing the chances of success of a movement (Zald and McCarthy 1987). Conversely, the Political Process school (McAdam 1982) refutes this supposition. This study questions the polarity between these two views by showing how temporary elite funding from one set of elites can be used to alter social relations with local elites. It simultaneously posits that the temporal nature of elite support reduces the potential for control.

In other words, short-term state support on a one-shot basis (as was available through DWCRA) had less potential for generating dependencies of women on the state than continuous long-term state support, and this is true of any source of elite support. Furthermore, dependencies between poor women and elites in close geographical proximity must be first addressed. This is critical because the participation of poor women in larger forums of decision making would not be possible unless social relations within their villages change first. In terms of timing, challenging local elites is a necessary first step, while addressing other elites is a longer-term process.

This section examines who these elites are; the nature and implications of different forms of elite involvement; and the necessity, purpose, and extent of elite involvement.

At the village level, elites would include big land-lords, moneylenders, local traders and members of local government structures such as the village panchayat. Local elites consist of the upper castes and/or the upper classes (Kohli 1986). Village government personnel are influenced by other local elite interests and are less sympathetic to the concerns of poor women. Certainly, poor women viewed their relationship with local elites as coercive and oppressive and any form of collaboration with these elites was out of the question. The expressed short-term and long-term goals of collectives and organisations were, in fact, to alter the nature of women's relationships with local elites.

The altering of social and gender relations was to be accomplished through the promotion of self-sufficiency and economic self-reliance among women and increasing the material and informational resources available to women to create sustainable livelihoods. This would, in the first place, reduce their dependence on moneylenders, landlords, and upper castes for employment and credit. It would also allow them to improve their skills increase their assets, and thereby increase opportunities for work and employment. Further, the creation of a separate space for women in the form of a women's collective would allow this new organisational entity (the collective) to articulate the needs of poor women and influence decision making at the village level.

This strategy adopted by organisers was simultaneously an acknowledgement on their part of the need for local organisation (though not necessarily formal) in order for women to change the social and economic relations in their villages.

This acknowledgement was one of devolution of power and decision making to the village-level community where the women's collective would be given a central role.

The second set of elites are those at the district, state, and national levels: officials/personnel in banks, funding agencies, research institutes universities, government agencies, and petty traders, and industrialists. These elites wanted to promote women's participation in development and thereby increase the economic contribution of poor women. The reason behind their collaboration was twofold: to integrate women into the market economy and to increase the legitimacy of state programmes that were hitherto unsuccessful.

It is apt to mention that the basic aim of SSP organisations was to increase women's decision-making capacities at all levels. However, the first step would be to change the local relations within the village community between women and local elites and then increase their decision-making capacities at higher levels. The first strategy adopted by the collectives and the organisations was to provide women with ways to obtain credit through the creation of a parallel credit system, i.e., savings and credit groups run by women themselves, thereby eliminating their dependence on moneylenders. The goal of creating a parallel, informal, credit system was largely accomplished between 1988 and 1992 by all organisations in the SSP.

This credit pool was run and operated by each collective, thereby protecting their funds from control by local elites (landlords, bankers, moneylenders) or from other oppressive structures within women's families (that of male family members— brothers, siblings, husbands, sons, fathers).

Once a pool of flexible funds had been created, the next step was to fund women's economic activities through leveraging additional government funds and bank loans to create jobs for women and provide them with a regular income source. This would decrease the dependence of women on seasonal wages received from agricultural labour performed for landlords and the accompanying vulnerability experienced by individual women due to uncertainty of the availability of this type of part-time, intermittent employment.

It would also allow women more freedom to participate in meetings and give them greater autonomy in decision making within their homes. The next stage would be to increase the decision-making power of the women's collective and participation in developmental activities at the village level, thereby ensuring chat all village level development is not influenced solely by landlords, upper castes and other local elites. This goal, however, would be difficult to achieve if women were dependent on moneylenders and landlords for credit and their livelihoods.

The reduction of such dependencies would be essential. The collective, too, had to be strengthened economically for this last goal to be achieved. By building the economic strength of women's groups through government subsidies and bank loans, the money from this set of elites could be used by women to assert themselves with local elites, as well as with men within their families. This was the strategy adopted to change social and economic relations between poor women and local elites.

In case of the second set of elites, the voluntary organisations mainly dealt with the state and banks. To a slightly lesser extent, outside funding agencies were also involved in providing funds for networking activities of the SSP. Consequently, women would receive their funds initially through time-bound loans from banks and one-time subsidies from government development agencies to initiate income-generation activities and to consolidate their collectives.

Finally, through the creation of federations of women's collectives and women's organisations, simultaneous efforts would be directed towards changing policies at district, state, and even national levels.

For this to occur the capacity of organisations and of collectives both had to be strengthened. The aim was to increase the bargaining power of women as a group and to provide them with the exposure necessary to articulate their concerns to the state and other formal institutions.

Limitations

In fact, failure of the theoretical framework of the Resource Mobilisation school to fully explain the role of incentives in the analysis of a social movement such as this lies in their not rooting their analysis firmly in the material conditions and, therefore, the class and gender status of movement participants. The focus on individual rationality is linked to the dual emphasis placed on material incentives for individuals to participate in movements and the capacity of organisations to mobilise resources.

Remarkably, Resource Mobilisation school

simultaneously lays too much stress on the material aspects of the movement actors and organisations and too little on the values put forth by social movements. In this case, while one major dimension of this movement was the initiative to seek resources, other aspects such as the moral or ideological ones were equally significant.

Ideological considerations that emerged as important counteracting forces here included a commitment to decentralised processes, the autonomy of organisations and collectives, non-hierarchical structures, and the self-reliance of poor communities. Looking at how organisations defined their mission, we see that organisational goals were several, going well beyond economic justice—such as uplifting women's social status; increasing the decision-making capabilities of people in the community and of poor women to shape development in their communities; changing social relations between poor women, men, and other social groups in the village; supporting women's networks and collectives; building the strength of women's groups; fighting for the equality and increased visibility of women; fighting caste, superstition, police oppression, and alcoholism; and issues that can be broadly defined as spanning the realm of concerns around social justice and not mere economic equality.

It is pertinent to note that contemporary social movement theory fails to explain third world women's movements. These theories are based on movements in the West and those which took place in the 1960s. In their very choice of the study of movements whose constituents typically belong to the middle class—such as the bourgeois feminist movements, the environmental movement, and movements based on identity politics in general or whose constituents belong to the organised labour force—social movements theorists have failed to make visible the agency of those who belong to the informal or unorganised sector in the third world or those who are only partly employed or unemployed in the first world.

The conclusions derived from the study of movements that have been defined as more visible tend to be biased to the extent that they validate formal or large organisations as more successful.

Most movement theorists greet the notion of decentralised and flexible forms of organisation with suspicion, associating assumptions of ineffectiveness and the movement organisations affiliated with them. While it is conceded that these SMOs are more participatory, they are simultaneously viewed as weak or lacking in focus. Part of this fallacy is the tendency of theory to focus on structure and not processes of learning and interaction.

The emphasis in social movement literature on the more visible, formal organisational structures has led to a misguided validation of these organisational forms and to predetermined conclusions that only such structures are successful. In embracing the notion that movement organisations are a direct and simple reflection of societal and economic conditions, these theories validate the very structures and institutions that movement actors typically are engaged in challenging.

By labeling formal large organisations as successful they render invisible the struggles of millions of people especially women, in India alone and even larger numbers of these engaged in community-based struggles around the world.

7

Notable Social Movements

"A man of a right spirit is not a man of narrow and private views, but is greatly interested and concerned for the good of the community to which he belongs, and particularly of the city or village in which he resides, and for the true welfare of the society of which he is a mem-ber."

—*Jonathan Edwards*

As is well known every society is infested with evils and problems. To curb these many social movements started in different parts of the world in different phases of history. No exaggeration, more information and awareness prove instrumental in leading social movements. In the modern day knowledge society, many social movements are being launched.

In this chapter we will introduce you to some such movements.

I. BLACK CONSCIOUSNESS MOVEMENT (BCM)

The Black Consciousness Movement (BCM) was a grassroots anti-Apartheid activist movement that emerged in South Africa in the mid-1960s out of the political vacuum created by the jailing and banning of the African National Congress and Pan Africanist Congress leadership after the Sharpeville

Massacre in 1960. The BCM represented a social movement for political consciousness.

> "Black Consciousness origins were deeply rooted in Christianity. In 1966, the Anglican Church under the incumbent, Archbishop Robert Selby Taylor, convened a meeting which later on led to the foundation of the University Christian Movement (UCM). This was to become the vehicle for Black Consciousness."

The BCM attacked what they saw as traditional white values, especially the 'condescending' values of white people of liberal opinion. They refused to engage white liberal opinion on the pros and cons of black consciousness, and emphasized the rejection of white monopoly on truth as a central tenet of their movement. While this philosophy at first generated disagreement amongst black anti-Apartheid activists within South Africa, it was soon adopted by most as a positive development.

As a result, there emerged a greater cohesiveness and solidarity amongst black groups in general, which in turn pro black consciousness to the forefront of the anti-Apartheid struggle within South Africa. The BCM's policy of perpetually challenging the dialectic of Apartheid South Africa as a means of conscientizing Black brought it into direct conflict with the full force of the security apparatus of the Apartheid regime. "Black man, you are on your own" became the rallying cry as mushrooming activity committees implemented what was to become a relentless campaign of challenge to what was then referred to by the BCM as 'the System'. It eventually sparked a confrontation on June 16, 1976 in the Soweto uprising, when at least 200 people were killed by the South African Security Forces, as students marched to protest the use of the Afrikaans language in African schools. Unrest spread like wildfire throughout the country. The Black revolution in South Africa had begun.

However, although it successfully implemented a system of comprehensive local committees to facilitate organized resistance, the BCM itself was decimated by security action taken against its leaders and social programs. By June 19, 1976, 123 key members had been banned and confined to remote rural districts. In 1977 all BCM related organizations were banned, many of its leaders arrested, and their social programs dismantled under provisions of the newly Implemented Internal Security Amendment Act. In September 1977, its banned National Leader, Steve Biko, was murdered while in the custody of the South African Security Police.

Important Figures in the Movement

- Steve Biko - founder
- Bennie Khoapa
- Mapetla Mohapi
- Malusi Mpumluana
- Thamsanga Mnyele - artist
- Rubin Phillip - cleric
- Barney Pityana
- Mamphela Ramphele - female political activist
- Mthuli ka Shezi - playwright
- Barney Simon - founder of The Market Theatre

Related Groups

- Azanian People's Organisation (AZAPO)
- Black Allied Worker's Union
- Black People's Convention
- Négritude, a literary movement in francophone Africa
- Neo Black Movement of Africa
- Socialist Party of Azania (SOPA)
- South African Student Organization

The Black Consciousness Movement started to develop during the late 1960s, and was led by Steve Biko, a black medical student, and Barney Pityana. During this period, the ANC had committed to an armed struggle through its military wing Umkhonto we Sizwe, but this small guerrilla army was neither able to seize and hold territory in South Africa nor to win significant concessions through its efforts. The ANC had been banned by apartheid leaders, and although the famed Freedom Charter remained in circulation in spite of attempts to censor it, for many students the ANC had disappeared.

The term Black Consciousness stems from American educator W.E.B. Du Bois's evaluation of the double consciousness of American black's being taught what they feel inside to be lies about the weakness and cowardice of their race. Du Bois echoed Civil War era black nationalist Martin Delany's insistence that black people take pride in their blackness as an important step in their personal liberation. This line of thought was also reflected in the Pan Africanist, Marcus Garvey, as well as Harlem Renaissance philosopher Alain Locke and in the salons of the Nardal sisters in Paris.

Biko's understanding of these thinkers was further shaped through the lens of postcolonial thinkers such as Frantz Fanon, Léopold Senghor, and Aimé Césaire. Biko reflects the concern for the existential struggle of the black person as a human being, dignified and proud of his blackness, in spite of the oppression of colonialism (see Négritude). The aim of this global movement of black thinkers was to restore black consciousness and African consciousness, which they felt had been suppressed under colonialism.

It is pertinent to note that part of the insight of the Black Consciousness Movement was in understanding that black liberation would not only come from imagining and fighting for structural political changes, as older movements like the ANC did, but also from psychological transformation in the minds of black people themselves.

This analysis suggested that to take power, black people had to believe in the value of their blackness. That is, if black people believed in democracy, but did not believe in their own value, they would not truly be committed to gaining power.

Along these lines, Biko saw the struggle to restore African consciousness as having two stages, "Psychological liberation" and "Physical liberation". While at times Biko embraced the non-violent tactics of Mahatma Gandhi and Martin Luther King, this was not because Biko fully embraced their spiritually-based philosophies of non-violence. Rather, Biko knew that for his struggle to give rise to physical liberation, it was necessary that it exist within the political and military realities of the apartheid regime, in which the armed power of the white government outmatched that of the black majority. Therefore Biko's non-violence may be seen more as a tactic than a personal conviction.

However, along with political action, a major component of the Black Consciousness Movement was its Black Community Programs, which included the organization of community medical clinics, aiding entrepreneurs, and holding "consciousness" classes and adult education literacy classes. Another important component of psychological liberation was to embrace blackness by insisting that black people lead movements of black liberation. This meant rejecting the fervent "non-racialism" of the ANC in favor of asking whites to understand and support, but not to take leadership in, the Black Consciousness Movement.

A parallel can be seen in the United States, where student leaders of later phases of SNCC, and black nationalists such as Malcolm X, rejected white participation in organizations that intended to build black power. While the ANC viewed white participation in its struggle as part of enacting the non-racial future for which it was fighting, the Black Consciousness view was that even well-intentioned white people often reenacted the paternalism of the society in which they lived. This view held that in a profoundly racialized society, black people had to first liberate themselves and gain psychological, physical and political power for themselves before "non-racial" organizations could truly be non-racial.

In fact, Biko's BCM had much in common with other left-wing African nationalist movements of the time, such as Amilcar Cabral's PAIGC and Huey Newton's Black Panther Party.

Although the ANC and others opposed to apartheid had initially focused on non-violent campaigns, the brutality of the Sharpeville Massacre of March 21, 1960 caused many blacks to embrace the idea of violent resistance to apartheid. However, although the ANC's armed wing started its campaign in 1961, no victory was in sight by the time that Steve Biko was a medical student in the late nineteen-sixties. Even as the nation's leading opposition groups like the ANC proclaimed a commitment to armed struggle, their leaders had failed to organize a credible military effort.

If their commitment to revolution had inspired many, the success of the white regime in quashing it had dampened the spirits of many. It was in this context that black students, Biko most notable among them, began critiquing the liberal whites with whom they worked in anti-apartheid student groups, as well as the official non-racialism of the ANC.

They saw progress towards power as requiring the development of black power distinct from supposedly "non-racial groups." This new Black Consciousness Movement not only called for resistance to the policy of Apartheid, freedom of speech, and more rights for South African blacks who were oppressed by the white Apartheid regime, but also black pride and a readiness to make blackness, rather than simple liberal democracy, the rallying point of unapologetically black organizations. Importantly, the group defined black to include other "people of color" in South Africa, most notably the large number of South Africans of Indian descent.

The movement stirred many blacks to confront not only the legal but also the cultural and psychological realities of Apartheid, seeking "not black visibility but real black participation" in society and in political struggles. The gains this movement made were widespread across South Africa. Many black people felt a new sense of pride about being black as the movement helped to expose and critique the inferiority complex felt by many blacks at the time.

The group formed Formation Schools to provide leadership seminars, and placed a great importance on decentralization and autonomy, with no person serving as president for more than one year (although Biko was clearly the primary leader of the movement). Early leaders of the movement such as Bennie Khoapa, Barney Pityana, Mapetla Mohapi, and Mamphela Ramphele joined Biko in establishing the Black Community Programmes (BCP) in 1970 as self-help groups for black communities, forming out of the South African Council of Churches and the *Christian Institute*.

They also published various journals, including the

Black Review, *Black Voice*, *Black Perspective*, and *Creativity in Development*.

It is significant to note that on top of building schools and day cares and taking part in other social projects, the BCM through the BCP was involved in the staging of the large scale protests and workers strikes which gripped the nation in 1972 and 1973, especially in Durban.

Indeed, in 1973 the government of South Africa began to clamp down on the movement, claiming that their ideas of black development were treasonous, and virtually the entire leadership of SASO and BPC were banned. In late August and September 1974, after holding rallies in support of the Frelimo government which had taken power in Mozambique, many leaders of the BCM were arrested under the Terrorism Act and the Riotous Assemblies Act. Arrests under these laws allowed the suspension of the doctrine of habeas corpus, and many of those arrested were not formally charged until the next year, resulting in the arrest of the "Pretoria Twelve" and conviction of the "SASO nine", which included Maitshe Mokoape and Patrick Lekota.

These were the most prominent among various public trials which gave a forum for members of the BCM to explain their philosophy and to describe the abuses that had been inflicted upon them. Far from crushing the movement, this led to its wider support among black and white South Africans.

The Soweto Riots and After

The Black Consciousness Movement heavily supported the protests against the policies of the apartheid regime which led to the Soweto riots in June 1976. The protests began when it was decreed that black students be forced to learn Afrikaans, and that many secondary school classes were to be taught in that language. This was another encroachment against the black population, which generally spoke indigenous languages like Zulu and Xhosa at home, and saw English as offering more prospects for mobility and economic self-sufficiency than did Afrikaans.

And the notion that Afrikaans was to define the national identity stood directly against the BCM principle of the development of a unique black identity. The protest began as a non-violent demonstration before police opened fire on the crowd, killing hundreds of youths.

The government's efforts to suppress the growing movement led to the imprisonment of Steve Biko, who became a symbol of the struggle. Biko died in police custody on September 12, 1977. It should be noted that Steve Biko was a non-violent activist, even though the movement he helped start eventually took up violent resistance. White newspaper editor Donald Woods supported the movement and Biko, whom he had befriended, by leaving South Africa and exposing the truth behind Biko's death at the hands of police by publishing the book *Biko*.

One month after Biko's death, the South African government declared 17 groups associated with the Black Consciousness Movement to be illegal. Following this, many members joined more concretely political and tightly-structured parties such as the ANC, which used underground cells to maintain their organizational integrity despite banning by the government.

And it seemed to some that the key goals of Black Consciousness had been attained, in that black identity and psychological liberation were growing. Nonetheless, in the months following Biko's death, activists continued to hold meetings to discuss resistance. Along with members of the BCM, a new generation of activists who had been inspired by the Soweto riots and Biko's death were present, including Bishop Desmond Tutu. Among the organizations that formed in these meetings to carry the torch of Black Consciousness was the Azanian People's Organization (AZAPO) which persists to this day.

Almost immediately after the formation of AZAPO in 1978, its chairman, Ishmael Mkhabela, and secretary, Lybon Mabasa were detained under the Terrorism Act. In the following years, other groups sharing Black Consciousness principles formed, including the Congress of South African Students (COSAS), Azanian Student Organization (AZASO) and the Port Elizabeth Black Civic Organization (PEBCO).

While many of these organizations still exist in some form, some evolved and could no longer be called parts of the Black Consciousness Movement. And as the influence of the Black Consciousness Movement itself waned, the ANC was returning to its role as the clearly leading force in the resistance to white rule. Still more former members of the Black Consciousness Movement continued to join the ANC, including Thozamile Botha from PEBCO.

Others formed new groups. For instance, in 1980, Pityana formed the Black Consciousness Movement of Azania (BCMA), an avowedly Marxist group which used AZAPO as its political voice. Curtis Nkondo from AZAPO and many members of AZASO and the Black Consciousness Media Workers Association joined the United Democratic Front (UDF). Many groups published important newsletters and journals, such as the *Kwasala* of the Black Consciousness Media Workers and the London based BCMA journal, *Solidarity*.

And beyond these groups and media outlets, the Black Consciousness Movement had an extremely broad legacy, even as the movement itself was no longer represented by a single organization. While the Black Consciousness Movement itself spawned an array of smaller groups, many people who came of age as activists in the Black Consciousness Movement did not join them.

Instead, they joined a other organizations, including the ANC, the Unity Movement, the Pan Africanist Congress, the United Democratic Front and trade and civic unions. The Black Consciousness Movement's most-lasting legacy is as an intellectual movement.

The weakness of theory in and of itself to mobilize constituencies can be seen in AZAPO's inability to win significant electoral support in modern-day South Africa. But the strength of the ideas can be seen in the diffusion of Black Consciousness language and strategy into nearly every corner of black South African politics.

In fact, these ideas helped make the complexity of the South African black political world, which can be so daunting to the newcomer or the casual observer, into a strength. As the government tried to act against this organization or that one, people in many organizations shared the general ideas of the Black Consciousness Movement, and these ideas helped to organize action beyond any specific organizational agenda.

If the leader of this group or that one was thrown into prison, nonetheless, more and more black South Africans agreed on the importance of black leadership and active resistance. Partly as a result, the difficult goal of unity in struggle became more and more realized through the late nineteen-seventies and nineteen-eighties. Biko and the legacy of the Black Consciousness movement helped give the resistance a culture of fearlessness. And its emphasis on individual psychological pride helped ordinary people realize they could not wait for distant leaders (who were often exiled or in prison) to liberate them. As the ANC's formal armed wing Umkhonto weSizwe struggled to make gains, this new fearlessness became the basis of a new battle in the streets, in which larger and larger groups of ordinary and often unarmed people confronted the police and the army more and more aggressively.

If the ANC could not defeat the white government's massive army with small bands of professional guerrilla fighters, it was able to eventually win power through ordinary black peoples' determination to make South Africa ungovernable by a white government. What could not be achieved by men with guns was accomplished by teenagers throwing stones. While much of this later phase of the struggle was not undertaken under the formal direction of Black Consciousness groups per se, it was certainly fueled by the spirit of Black Consciousness. Kashy Singh(2005) had said that black people are equal to all other human beings

Even after the end of apartheid, Black Consciousness politics live on in community development projects and "acts of dissent" staged both to bring about change and to further develop a distinct black identity.

Controversies and Criticism

A balanced analysis of the results and legacy of the Black Consciousness Movement would no doubt find a variety of perspectives. A list of research resources is listed at the end of this section including Columbia University's Project on Black Consciousness and Biko's Legacy.

Criticisms of the Movement sometimes mirror similar observations of the Black Consciousness Movement in the United States. (See reference to Fredrickson's comparative work below). On one side, it was argued that the Movement would stagnate into black racialism, aggravate racial tensions and attract repression by the apartheid regime. Other detractors thought the Movement based heavily on student idealism, but with little grassroots support among the masses, and few consistent links to the mass trade-union movement.

Assessments of the movement (See Gerhard references below) note that it failed to achieve several of its key objectives. It did not bring down the apartheid regime, nor did its appeal to other non-white groups as "people of color" gain much traction. Its focus on blackness as the major organizing principle was very much downplayed by Nelson Mandela and his successors who to the contrary emphasized the multi-racial balance needed for the post-apartheid nation. The community programs fostered by the movement were very small in scope and were subordinated to the demands of protest and indoctrination. Its leadership and structure was essentially liquidated, and it failed to bridge the tribal gap in any large-scale way, although certainly small groups and individuals collaborated across tribes.

After much blood shed and property destroyed, critics charged that the Movement did nothing more than raise 'awareness' of some issues, while accomplishing little in the way of sustained mass organization, or of practical benefit for the masses. Some detractors also assert that Black consciousness ideas are out-dated, hindering the new multi-racial South Africa.

Defenders of the BCM by contrast held that charges of impracticality failed to grasp the universal power of an idea - the idea of freedom and liberation for blacks. This was Biko's reply to many of the Movement's critics. Indeed Biko rejected the "practicality" charge as an example of the compromises that hindered and delayed black liberation, saying in 1977: "We have been successful to the extent that we have diminished the element of fear in the minds of black people." See Columbia reference below.

Defenders of the movement argued that blackness was the best, most energetic organizing principle that was available at the time, in contrast to laborious legal, non-violent and petition based integrationist approach used by white dominated moderate groups.

Biko made no bones about the 'consciousness' aspect of the movement and in this limited respect he is similar to Huey P. Newton of the Black Panthers in the United States. What was important to Biko and other leaders, was not creating yet another political party or group squabbling over local spoils, but a fundamental mobilization and change in attitude and outlook of the black oppressed and destitute. Some contemporary BCM leaders claim that its principles are currently relevant and decry what they see as evidence of 'sellout' in the new South Africa.

It is pertinent to note that in comparison with the Black Power movement in the United States, the Black Consciousness movement felt little need to reconstruct any sort of golden cultural heritage. African linguistic and cultural traditions were alive and well in the country. Short stories published predominantly in Drum magazine had led to the 1950s being called the *Drum decade*, and future Nobel Prize winner Nadine Gordimer was beginning to become active. The fallout from the Sharpeville massacre led to many of those artists entering exile, but the political oppression of the resistance itself led to a new growth of black South African Literature.

In the 1970s, Staffrider magazine became the dominant forum for the publication of BC literature, mostly in the form of poetry and short stories. Book clubs, youth associations, and clandestine street-to-street exchange became popular. Various authors explored the Soweto riots in novels, including Miriam Tlali, Mothobi Mutloatse and Mbulelo Mzamane. But the most compelling force in Black Consciousness prose was the short story, now adapted to teach political morals. Mtutuzeli Matshoba famously wrote, "*Do not say to me that I am a man.*"

An important theme of Black Consciousness literature was the *rediscovery of the ordinary*, which can be used to describe the work of Njabulo Ndebele. However, it was in poetry that the Black Consciousness Movement first found its voice. In a sense, this was a modern update of an old tradition, since several of South Africa's African languages had long traditions of performed poetry. Sipho Sempala, Mongane Serote, and Mafika Gwala led the way, although Sempala turned to prose after Soweto. Serote wrote from exile of his internalization of the struggles, while Gwala's work was informed and inspired by the difficulty of life in his home township of Mpumalanga near Durban. These forerunners inspired a myriad of followers, most notably poet-performance artist Ingoapele Madingoane.

James Mathews was a part of the *Drum decade* who was especially influential to the Black Consciousness Movement. This poem gives an idea of the frustrations that blacks felt under apartheid:

Freedom's child
You have been denied too long

Fill your lungs and cry rage
Step forward and take your rightful place
You are not going to grow up knocking at the back door....

This poem by an unknown author has a rather confrontational look:

Kaffer man, Kaffer nation
Arise, arise from the kaffer
Prepare yourself for war!
We are about to start

Steve Biko the hero Mandlenkosi Langa's poem: "Banned for Blackness" also calls for black resistance :

Look up, black man, quit stuttering and shuffling
Look up, black man, quit whining and stooping
...raise up your black fist in anger and vengeance.

A main tenet of the Black Consciousness Movement itself was the development of black culture, and thus black literature. The cleavages in South African society were real, and the poets and writers of the BCM saw themselves as spokespersons for blacks in the country.

II. GLOBAL JUSTICE MOVEMENT

The Global Justice Movement is the broad globalized social movement opposing what is often known as "corporate globalization" and promoting equal distribution of economic resources. Its unifying theme is opposition to (what it perceives as) tyranny. A number of organizations and groups using this term have emerged at the beginning of this century - see links and references.

Movement of Movements

The Global Justice Movement describes the loose collection of individuals and groups—often referred to as a "movement of movements"—who advocate "fair trade" rules and are negative to current institutions of global economics such as the World Trade Organization.

The movement is often labeled the anti-globalization movement by the mainstream media. Those involved, however, frequently deny that they are "anti globalization," insisting that they support the globalization of communication and people and oppose only the global expansion of corporate power. The term further indicates an anti-capitalist and universalist perspective on globalization, distinguishing the movement from those opponents of globalization whose politics are based on a conservative defence of national sovereignty.

Important organizational pillars of the movement are Via Campesina, the family farmers' international; Peoples' Global Action, a loose collection of often youthful groups; Jubilee 2000, the Christian-based movement for relieving international debt; Friends of the Earth, the environmentalist international; and some think-tanks like Focus on the Global South and Third World Network. Participants include student groups, NGOs, trade unions, faith-based and peace groups throughout the world. A loose coordination of the movement is taking place on the Social Forums. However, although formal power is often situated in the global South, the resources of North-based NGOs give these disproportionate power to often informally marginalize popular organizations from the South.

Massive Protests

The movement is characterized by the massive citizen protests and alternative summits which have, for the last decade, accompanied most meetings of the G8, World Trade Organization, International Monetary Fund, and World

Bank. The movement came to the attention of many in the US when activists successfully used protests to shut down the 1999 WTO Ministerial in Seattle. This represented, however, just one of a series of massive Global Justice protests that have included protests at the 1988 World Bank/IMF meetings in Germany, "IMF riots" beginning in Lima in 1975, over cuts in the social safety-net presided over by IMF and other international organizations, and spreading through the world, and "water wars" in Bolivia and South Africa.

International Solidarity

The Global Justice Movement claims to place a significant emphasis on transnational solidarity uniting activists in the global South and global North. Some have argued that the World Social Forum is one excellent example of this emphasis, bringing activists together from around the world to focus on shared philosophy and campaigning. However others see the World Social Forum as dominated by Northern NGOs, donors and activists and argue that Southern representation is largely organized via Northern donors and their NGOs and that popular organizations in the global South are systematically marginalized or included in a deeply subordinated manner. For this reason many grassroots movements in the South boycott the forum and the NGOs that gate-keep representation at the forum or, in some instance, actively oppose it as just one more space of domination.

[*Source:* Wikipedia]

III. THE ZEITGEIST MOVEMENT

The Zeitgeist Movement (TZM) is a grassroots movement and online community. It describes itself as a sustainability advocacy organization, and is the official activist arm of

The Venus Project founded by industrial designer and social engineer Jacque Fresco. The Zeitgeist Movement was inspired by the social response from Peter Joseph's film *Zeitgeist: Addendum*, sequel to *Zeitgeist: The Movie*. It was *Zeitgeist: Addendum* which first introduced the Venus Project. A third film was released globally on January 15, 2011 called *Zeitgeist: Moving Forward*, which focuses on human behavior, technology, and rationality. The movement's website states that a distinction is made between the work of the movement and the issues raised in Peter Joseph's films in that the movement is not necessarily in advocacy of any issues raised in the films and exists on its own.

Concepts Advocated by the Zeitgeist Movement

The core idea advocated by TZM is an anti-capitalist system, replacing current civilization with a money-free and cybernated "resource-based economy". They promote replacing human labour with automation, government will be through collective participation of the public, aided by advanced cybernation. According to the movement, there will be no decision-making process, decisions are arrived at by using the scientific method, based on the carrying capacity of the Earth, rather than human opinions.

The replacement of human decision making by artificial intelligence is termed 'Social Cybernation'. Private property will not be abolished, but it will be become obsolete as culture grows, being replaced by "a system of universal access"

- Management of the Earth's natural resources: Once surveyed, the Earth's natural resources will no longer be privately owned. They will be managed according to general sustainability principles of preservation, recycling and optimization.

- No money, barter, trade or property: The monetary value of commodities does not represent the actual physical supply of natural resources, or their utilitarian value, which is integral to the success of the type of sustainable global society that the Zeitgeist Movement advocates. Income is a requirement for individuals to sustain life in a monetary system, so this in turn creates the need for commodities to be continuously bought and sold and for goods to be continuously produced, in order to make sure that the operation of social functions is maintained. This, combined with competition over market share, creates an abundance of goods that usually exceeds the demand for them, which in turn depletes natural resources and may create excessive waste. Furthermore, the profit motive inherent in a monetary system creates an incentive to increase profits regardless of the impact on human beings or the environment. When labor is displaced or outsourced, it either removes a laborer's source of sustenance, or takes advantage of inexpensive laborers. Certain manufacturers and corporations have been noted to contaminate the environment by dumping their by-products and waste materials instead of disposing of them properly, in order to save money. Other manufacturers have been known to take advantage of a process called planned obsolescence in order to increase sales of their products over time. With universal access to goods and services provided by a sustainable means of production based on resource availability, optimization and preservation, these problems of a monetary economy can be overcome.

- Automation: Machine automation is more productive than human labor and replaces the need for people to perform repetitive and tedious tasks.
- Technological unification of the Earth: Globally networked technological infrastructure is required to monitor planetary resources in real time, and theoretically make the most efficient use of them in solving planetary problems.
- Scientific method: Decision making regarding the methods of production, what goods and services are to be provided, city planning and resource optimization, preservation and recycling will be arrived at by analysing relevant trends and data, via use of the scientific method.
- Sustainable city systems: Utilizing a systems theory approach for a sustainable global society, city systems may act as microcosm to the global network of technological infrastructure. The city system can incorporate all manufacturing, goods and services that people will use on a daily basis within the city limits. The city system may also utilize a cybernetic central computer to monitor energy and resource supply, usage and other relevant data in real time, relaying this information to other city systems that make up the macrocosm of the technologically unified globe.

Phases of the Movement

Phase 1: Awareness Phase

As of 20 April 2010 (2010 -04-20) the Zeitgeist Movement

was in phase 1, consisting of collecting people, getting the movement's information out, and finding identification with other groups of individuals across all races, religions, and ethnicities. Phase 1 also consists of, but is not limited to, forming teams to create the infrastructure of the movement site, a communication team, and a development team. Another aspect of phase 1 is forming international chapters which are needed for creating the infrastructure for communication on a global level. The main objective of phase 1 is the need for more members, in order to make the existence of the movement relevant to the external world.

Phase 2: Project Phase

Phase 2 is the team action phase, which the movement is not in yet, where chapter projects are shared with the community. This collective understanding is needed for a synchronized approach for projects such as knowledgeable lecturers. This is also the phase for organized awareness projects which are anticipated to lead to the incubation of offshoot projects such as ending world hunger, disarmament (by choice, not force), and anti-militarism. This phase focuses on expansion of the teams which will lead to expansion of the group and the creation of a functional organization. The aim of phase 2 is the interconnection of these groups with interrelated and interdisciplinary focuses.

Phase 3: Action Phase

Phase 3 is where more assertive forms of activism will occur such as boycotts, fund raising, city construction and possibly instigating direct interaction with corporate and political organizations in the form of bio-social pressures.

Activities and Publications

Zeitgeist Day (Z-Day)

The Zeitgeist Movement holds an annual "Z-Day" in

March. The first Z-Day was on March 15, 2009 and the second on March 13, 2010. On this day, the Zeitgeist Movement has local gatherings to learn and share information with all interested individuals. In 2009 there were more than 450 events held in 70 countries around the world. In 2009, among other events, Peter Joseph and Jacque Fresco spoke to a sold-out crowd of around 900 at the Borough of Manhattan Community College for over two hours.

Media Project

According to a press release circulated to members on May 12, 2010, the Zeitgeist Media Project (ZMP) Beta was released. According to the press release the Media Project is an extension of the Communications Team.

Chapters

The Zeitgeist Movement members are organized into country/regional, state and city "sub"-chapters. Each chapter/ sub-chapter is hosted and maintained independently on its own domain, or in sub-domains from the Zeitgeist Movement's main site. The chapters are coordinated by individuals or groups of individuals who are well-versed in the movement's tenets and direction and have chosen to donate their time to help further its current goals. According to the Zeitgeist Movement July 2010 Newsletter, the Zeitgeist Movement has 46 official country chapters over 200 regional sub-chapters internationally. This includes all 50 official U.S. state chapters.

Radio Address

Peter Joseph delivers a weekly radio address (on hiatus as of 2011) broadcast every Wednesday on BlogTalkRadio. These broadcasts discuss the progress of the Zeitgeist Movement, hold interviews with various relevant personalities, provide information for the Zeitgeist Movement's chapters, and answer questions sent in by listeners/members. There are two other BlogTalkRadio shows that discuss the Zeitgeist Movement, a resource-based economy and the Venus Project. One is Z Radio, a weekly broadcast co-hosted by Thunder and Franklee, and produced by Shawn Hodgins. The other, known as V-Radio, is hosted by Neil Kiernan Stephenson (aka, VTV).

Reception

Media Reviews

On April 30, 2009, Rhonda Swan of the *Palm Beach Post* wrote:

> "Who can argue with such a movement? What we have never has worked for the benefit of society as a whole. How much longer can we really expect it to last? Isn't keeping our current system and expecting something different from what it's always given us insanity?"
>
> —*Palm Beach Post*

On March 17, 2009, Alan Feuer of the New York Times wrote:

> "The mission of the movement is the application of the scientific method for social change," Mr. Joseph announced by way of introduction. The evening, which began at 7 with a two-hour critique of monetary economics, became by midnight a utopian presentation of a money-free and computer-driven vision of the future, a wholesale reimagination of civilization, as if Karl Marx and Carl Sagan had hired John Lennon from his "Imagine" days to do no less than redesign the underlying structures of planetary life."
>
> —*New York Times*

From the same article:

> ""If this sounds vaguely like a disaster scenario out of "2001: A Space Odyssey," Mr. Fresco did not seem worried in the least. Machines are unemotional and unaggressive, unlike human beings, he told the crowd during the question-and-answer phase. "If you took your laptop and smashed it in front of 50 other laptops, trust me, none of them would care."

In June 2009, the German networking site StudiVZ shut down the Zeitgeist Movement's group, which reportedly had around ten thousand members, and sent a letter to the group's administrator stating that the reason for the ban was Anti-Semitic tendencies expressed by the group's members. The group has vehemently denied this accusation, particularly on the forum of The Zeitgeist Movement's website. Members stated that the accusation made an unfair association to groups which supported Jewish world domination conspiracy theories.

[*Source:* Wikipedia]

REFERENCES

Africana: The Encyclopedia of the African and African American Experience. edited by Kwame Anthony Appiah, Henry Louis Gates. Basic Civitas Books (1999), p. 250.

Alan Feuer (March 16, 2009). "They've Seen the Future and Dislike the Present". New York Times.

Alex Callinicos, *An Anti-Capitalist Manifesto*. London: Polity, 2003.

Amatoritsero, *The Black Consciousness Movement in South African Literature,* (Godwin) Ede

David Solnit, *Globalize Liberation: How to Uproot the System and Build a Better World'.' San Francisco: City Lights, 2003.*

della Porta, D. 2005. "The Social Bases of the Global Justice Movement: Some Theoretical Reflections and Empirical Evidence from the First European Social Forum." Civil Society and Social Movements Programme Paper No. 21.Geneva:

UNRISD (United Nations Research Institute for Social Development).

Donatella della Porta, *The Global Justice Movement: Cross-national And Transnational Perspectives*. New York: Paradigm, 2006.

Doug Killam. *The Companion to African Literatures*. Indiana University Press (2001) (Section titled *Apartheid*), p. 29-47.

Feuer, Alan (March 17, 2009). "They've Seen the Future and Dislike the Present". *The New York Times*. http://www.nytimes.com/2009/03/17/nyregion/17zeitgeist.html?_r=1.

Gail M. Gerhart, Black Power in South Africa: The Evolution of an Ideology (1979).

Gelder, Melinda, *Meeting the Enemy, Becoming a Friend*. Boulder: Bauu Press, 2006.

George M. Fredrickson, White Supremacy: A Comparative Study of American and South African History (1981).

Hadden, J. Tarrow, S., *Spillover or Spillout? The Global Justice Movement in the United States after 9/11*, Mobilization, 2007, VOL 12; NUMB 4, pages 359-376, online

Hochman, Steve (3 August 2010). "Natacha Atlas Illuminates the Shifting Global Zeitgeist". *Spinner News*. http://www.spinnermusic.co.uk/2010/08/03/natacha-atlas-illuminates-the-shifting-global-zeitgeist/. Retrieved 10 August 2010.

Jacque Fresco "City Systems", Cybernetic Government *The Venus Project*

Jai Sen, Peter Waterman, *World Social Forum - Challenging Empires*. Black Rose 2008

John Brewer, *After Soweto: An Unfinished Journey*. Oxford: Clarendon Press, (1986) ch. 4

John Walton, David Seddon, Free Markets & Food Riots. Blackwell 1994

Kwasi Wiredu, William E. Abraham, Abiola Irele, Ifeanyi A. Menkiti. (eds.) *Companion to African Philosophy*. Blackwell Publishing (2003) p. 213.

Mary Amanda Axford. *Mary of Many Colors: Book Review: Biko, by Donald Woods* Accessed on November 22, 2009.

Michael Lobban. *White Man's Justice: South African Political Trials in the Black Consciousness Era*. New York: Oxford University Press (1996)

Nigel Gibson. *Black Consciousness 1977-1987; The Dialectics of Liberation in South Africa* Accessed on December 1, 2005.

Rhonda Swan (April 30, 2009). "COLUMN: A dream worth having". The Palm Beach Post. http://www.palmbeachpost.com/opinion/content/opinion/epaper/2009/04/30/swancol_0501.html#. Retrieved May 4, 2009.

8

Social Reform Movements

Generally, many social evils prevail in societies. Weak and poor are more vulnerable to these evils. Indian society, example has been infested with social evils like child marriage, untouchability, female foeticide and infanticide etc. In different phases of Indian history many charismatic social leaders emerged and launched social reform movements.

In this chapter we will introduce you to some of such movements.

It has been an established fact that Christian Missionaries were one of the first to have created conditions of self-awareness against exploitation. Many of them started working with the lower castes and tribes and succeeded in converting large groups. By 1903 more than 5000 toddy tappars were converted to Christianity in the Madras Presidency. With the active support of the British Raj the missionaries were not only able to expand their evangelical, medical and welfare measures but were also successful in securing for their converts basic civil rights and employments in public services.

It is apt to mention here that the reform movements among the upper-caste/classes also created conditions of self-awareness among the deprived sections. The Brahmo

Samaj and the Arya Samaj that emerged in the 19th centuries were concerned with two major programmes -the emancipation of women and the amelioration of the depressed classes.

While the former concerned itself mainly with the upper classes and castes the latter related itself mainly to the problem of the untouchables. Under the leadership of Keshab Chandra Sen,the Brahmo Samaj organized education and welfare programmes for the untouchables. The Arya Samaj took greater interest in the upliftment of the untouchables.

It started the Shuddhi movement in 1891 to reconvert the low caste Christian and Muslim converts back to Hindusim.It gave the untouchables the right to wear the sacred thread, the symbol of twice born status and also established educational institutions for the benefit of the untouchables.

As a significant development, the Servants of Indian Society founded by G.K. Gokhale in 1905 had the amelioration of the depressed classes as one of its objectives. In Bombay V R Shinde founded the Depressed Classes Mission in 1906 and established education institutions. These reform movements were led by western educated upper class intellectuals who hoped of a renaissance and formulated a liberal and egalitarian ideology.

ARYA SAMAJ

Basically, the Arya Samaj is a reform movement and religious/ social organization which was formally established in Bombay in 1875 by Swami Dayananda Saraswathi (1824-1883). He was an adamant follower, exponent, and practitioner of the Vedas—the unadulterated Truth as handed down from Guru to disciple since the beginning of time. Swami

Dayananda had absolutely no craving for worldly applause and was completely unconcerned and unperturbed by the censure of the superstitious, the ignorant, and the selfish.

Swami Dayanada spoke the Truth and practiced it too. In 1863 he emerged preaching against idolatry and started Sanskrit classes. In 1872 he came into cantact with Keshub Chandra Sen, a Brahmo reformer and other Brahmo leaders.

It exerted a radical change in him which led him to turn from Sanskrit to the popular language Hindi for spreading his ideals. In 1875 he went to Bombay for preaching his ideals and there he enjoyed a warm support at the hands of great social reformer Mahadev Govind Ranade in the campaign against idolatry and other evil practices. In the same year he founded Arya Samaj in Bombay.

Two years later in 1877 he shifted the headquarters of the samaj to Lahore and carried on his activities. The word Arya means a noble human being—one who is thoughtful and charitable, who thinks good thoughts and does good actions—he or she is an Arya. The universal Arya Samaj (Vishwa Arya Samaj) is a gathering of such people.

Swami Dayanada founded Arya Samaj on two basic tenets. these include:

- Infallible authority of the Vedas
- Monotheism.

Dayananda has explained these two principles in his book Satyartha Prakash that he published in 1874 from Allahabad. He held the Vedas only as the infallible authority of Hinduism. He believed that four Vedas are words of God. They are absolutely free from error and or an authority into themselves. They do not stand in need of any other book to uphold their authority. They comprise what is known as the Samhita.

However he cautioned that they might be held authoritative only in so far as they conform to the teachings of the Vedas. If there is any passage in these works opposed to Vedic injunctions it can entirely be rejected. He held Brahman as the most higher or paramatman the supreme spirit who permeates the whole universe; who is personification of sat-chit-ananda who is omniscient, formless, all pervading, unborn, infinite almighty who creates, sustains and dissolves the universe and who awards all souls the fruit of their deeds in accordance with the requirements of absolute justice. One can attain salvation through the worship of God.

In fact, there are three elements—stuti, *prarthna* and *upasana stuti* or glorification consists in praising the attributes and powers of God with a view in fixing them in our minds and cultivating love towards God. Prarthana is praying to God for the gift of the highest knowledge and other blessings. Upasana or communion consists in conforming to the Divine spirit in purity and holiness and in feeling the presence of the Deity in our heart through the practice of Yoga which enables us to have direct cognition of God. He believed that revitalization of the Hindu religion and society could be achieved by purifying the religion and uniting Hindu society.

He believed that the purification of religion could be achieved by purging the religion of its impurities like polytheism and idolatry. So he attacked these two things and advocated a monotheism worship of the formless Brahman. For uniting the Hindus and strengthening the society Swami Dayananda also started three movements -

shuddi, sanghatan and education and geared the Arya Samaj to carry on these movements unceasingly. Shuddi is a ceremony by which the Non-Hindus the fallen, the outcastes, the converts and the externals were taken into the Hindu fold.

By this ceremony the Arya Samaj not only invested the depressed classes and untouchables with the sacred thread and gave them equal status with other Hindus but also reclaimed many Hindus who were formerly converted to Islam and Christianity. The word sanghatan means union. Therefore it implies in the programme of the Arya Samaj the organization of Hindus for self-defence. The Arya Samaj declared that no Hindu should take lying down the insults hurled against his religion by the preachers of other religion. The Hindu should cultivate a militant spirit and should take up the challenge. The Arya samaj embarked upon the programme of national education for the Hindus.

Swami Dayananda emphasized the need for a national education throughout his career. In every place he visited he pleaded for the establishment of Sanskrit schools and the teaching of Vedas. Swami Dayananda desired that Hindu society emerges as a moral society. So he preached that the Hindu should observe dharma in their life. Dharma is a practice of equitable justice together with that of truthfulness in word, deed and thought and like virtues as embodied in the Vedas.

He believed in the doctrines of Karma and rebirth; stressed the old ideals of brahmacharya and sanyasa insisted on the efficacy of samskars and rite of upanayana and homa upheld the sanctity of the cow, condemned animal sacrifices, ancestor worship, pilgrimages, priest-craft, untouchability and child marriage as lacking Vedic sanction. After his death the leaders of the Arya Samaj accepted his sayings and teachings as the doctrines of Samaj and tried to spread the activities of the samaj all over the country.

Basic Tenets

1. God is the original source of all true knowledge and all that is known by the physical sciences.
2. God is existen, intelligent and blissful. He is formless, almighty,just,merciful,unborn and endless,unchangeable, incomparable, the support and master of all. He is ominpresent and and the maker of the universe. He alone is worthy of worship.
3. The Vedas are the scriptures of all true knowledge. It is the duty of all Aryas to read them, hear them being read and teach them to others.
4. One should always be ready to accept truth and give up untruth.
5. All acts should be performed in accordance with Dharma, after deliberating what is right and wrong.
6. The primary object of Arya Samaj is to do good to the world by promoting physical, spiritual and social good of everyone.
7. Our conduct towards all should be guided by love ,righteousness and justice.
8. We should dispel ignornace and promote knowledge.
9. One should see one's own greatest welfare as residing in the welfare of others.
10. One should regard oneself under restriction to follow the rules of society calculated to promote the well being of all, while one should be free in matters of individual welfare.

SATYA SODHAK SAMAJ

Mahatma Jyotirao Phule, though a Mali by caste and of comparatively little education started the association called the Satyashodhak Samaj in Pune 1873 for asserting the worth of man irrespective of caste. He demanded representation of all classes of the Hindus in all the local bodies, in services and institutions and also established a primary school for the so-called untouchables in Poona. Tracing the evolution of the Non-Brahmin movement in Western India from 1873 to 1930 the Satya Sodhak Samaj has been described by Gail Omvedt as a cultural revolt in a colonial society. But there is a clear distinction between Satyasodhak movement, which was essentially a socio-religious movement, and the non-Brahmin movement, which was predominantly a political movement.

Basic Tenets

In fact, Satya Sodhak Samaj put a ban on discussion of political questions. Any Sudra was free to join the Satya sodhak samaj as member but people belonging to the upper castes were either listed as friends of samaj or admitted as members after sometime only when other members of the Samaj were convinced about their outlook and actions. The sathya sodhak movement attacked the Brahmin priests who insisted on acting as intermediaries between God and devotees.

They believed that there was no need for any intermediary in matters of religion and refused to recognize the traditional role of the Brahmins as custodians of Hindu religion or interpreters of scriptures. They also opposed the stranglehold of the bureaucracy dominated by the Brahmins in their times.

Phule often complained that the Brahmin bureaucrats

were responsible for misleading the white rulers and hence they should be replaced by non-Brahmins who would be better informed about and more sympathetic to the peasants in rural areas. They totally rejected the Vedic tradition and the Aryan heritage. He regarded the Aryans as conquerors and destroyers of the indigenous non-Aryan culturo.

He launched a vigorous attack on the Vedas. He made fun of the puranas and ridiculed those who believed in the absurd stories narrated by their Brahmin authors. The Satya Sodhak movement continued to emphasize the role of education in facilitating social change. Phule campaigned against the increasing habit of drinking liquor and urged the Poona Municipal Council not to permit the opening of liquor shops.

He tried to persuade people to give up drinking and spend their money on buying books. The Satya Shodhak movement in 19th century was essentially a socio-religious reform movement that was transformed by Shahu Chhatrapati into a powerful Non-Brahmin movement, which sought to bring a change into a power structure. His ideas are now being rejuvenated in Uttar Pradesh by BSP.

RAM KRISHNA MISSION

Shri Rama Krishna Paramahansa is a unique figure in the history of Hinduism. He advocated the entire orbit of Hinduism and not simply by a segment of it such as Theism or Vedism.

He viewed God to be both personal and impersonal. He laid equal emphasis on both the householder's life of good works and the sanyasi's life of renunciation and yoga like a true Hindu, he gave free scope to the individual variations in the kingdom of spirit. And again like a true Hindu he held that all religions were branches of the same tree. He demonstrated this truth in his own life by going through the sadhanas of Islam and Christianity as well as Hinduism.

Without much education and scholarship, he understood and exposed the truths of Hindu scriptures. He traveled the entire region experience by his own tapas and confirmed by his own personal testimony the truths of Hindu scriptures. His practice of spiritual realizations of different creeds led him to discover certain basic truths.

Basic Tenets

1. Realization of God is the essence of religion and the end and aim of human existence. All religious works, discussion discourse and sermons will automatically stop when realizations end.
2. To a man who has realized God all religions are paths that lead to the same goal. The substance is one only the names are different. He who is called Krishna in Vaishnavisms is called Shiva in Saivism, Adyashadti in Shakta, Jesus in Christianity and Allah in Islam.
3. The realization of God can be attained through gnana and bhakti. The latter is to be preferred. The former namely the path of knowledge is difficult because one has to acquire a high degree of purity and self-control before one can tread that path whereas the latter namely the path of devotion is easy because purity and self-control come of their own accord when once a man begins to love God.
4. Shri Ramakrishna Paramahansas religion is a practical one. It is not concerned with the

metaphysical subtitles philosophical discussions and interpretations of spiritual messages. It is concerned only with the realization of God through spiritual experience. That is why he did not condemn idol-worship. He regarded it as a mean to an end in itself.

5. Love of God should take precedence not only to knowledge but also of good works. Social service is no-doubt necessary and good but it should be a part of divine service.

SRI NARAYANGURU DHARMA PARIPALANA SABHA

It is pertinent to note that from 1812 until almost the close of the century, though political life was characterized by inactivity and society presented an outward calmness, subversive forces were forming and developing. This current of social transformation gradually led Kerala into the mainstream of political struggle for freedom and responsible government in the 20th century.

The important outcome of this ferment was the awakening of the masses especially the lower orders in the Hindu society, against social injustice and evils. This awakening found articulation in Kerala towards the last quarter of the 19th century. In the princely states of Kochi and Travancore, the hold of the caste system was even more suffocating. Until the 20th century, governmental positions were denied to lower castes and non-Hindus.It was a protest movement that originated among the scheduled castes. The SNDP movement originated among the Izhavas (todday-tappers) of Kerala in the late nineteenth century. Izhavas were regarded as unapproachable in the traditional caste hierarchy. For instance, they had to stay way thirty-four feet from the Nambudiri Brahmins.

They suffered from many disabilities, both civic and ritual: they were not allowed to worship in the temples of caste Hindus or to bathe in the tanks of caste Hindus. Toddy-tapping was considered to be a defiling occupation, their women were to required to cover their breasts and they could neither wear any footwear not build pucca houses. Shri Narayana Guru, the great Hindu saint and social reformer spearheaded one of the most important social reform movements.

The Guru was born in 1856 in the Ezhava community, which had a status far below that of the Nambudiris. He fearlessly criticized and campaigned against the rigors of the caste system, the Brahmin hegemony and the numerous social disabilities of the Ezhavas and other lower castes. Soon Shri Narayana Guru became the rallying point for the Ezhavas and Thiyyas to unite and organize.

It is pertinent to note that Shri Narayana Dharma Paripalana Yogam (SNDP), literally the society for the propagation of moral teaching of Shri Narayana came into being 15th May 1903. Within a short period, the Guru and Yogam drew towards them a brilliant band of dedicated workers, including the poet Kumaran Asan, whose efforts constitute an eloquent testimony to what a community, submitted to centuries of tyranny, can do and achieve through unity, realism and organism.Shri Narayana was, however, no sectarian philosopher and leader.

A programme of action founded upon such sublime humanism and social purpose was not destined to remain confined to one caste only; it soon became the philosophy of Hindu reformation, encompassing all castes, including the Brahmin. The Shri Narayana Movement had developed as a reformative and reaffirmative movement within the Hindu religion. The temple that Sree Narayana Gure consecrated to Lord Siva, the Mirror consecration at Kalavancode and the like were against the Hindu upper class domination. Yet this move did not spread among the Dalits.

In effect, it was an attempt to reform the caste and the religion. He was responsible for a thorough transformation on the style of life involving new religious beliefs, ritual and outlook. He provided and ideology or withdrawal and self-organization that raised the self-respect, honor and worth of individuals. It was an ideology of protest against the Brahmincal value system of hierarchy and pollution. Swamy established a parallel source of legitimacy with his institutions of temples, priests, monks and monasteries.

PEASANT MOVEMENTS

It is apt to mention that peasants and artisans were the worst exploited section of Indian society. Colonial economic policies, the new land revenue system, the colonial administrative and judicial system and the ruin of handicrafts leading to the overcrowding of land ,transformed the agrarian structure and impoverished the peasantary.

In the vast zamindari areas the peasants were left to the mercies of the zamindar who rack-rented them and compelled them to pay illegal dues and perform beggar. In the ryotwari areas, the government itself levied heavy land revenue. This forced the peasants to borrow money from the moneylenders.

Gradually over large areas the actual cultivators were reduced to the status of tenants at will, share croppers and landless labourers while their lands, crops and cattle passed into the hands to landlords, trader moneylenders and such peasants.

When the peasants could take it no longer they resisted against the oppression and exploitation and they found whether their target was the indigenous exploiter or the colonial administration that their real enemies after the barriers were down was the colonial state.

In 1930s nation wide awakening of peasants was largely the result of the combination of particular economic and political developments.

- The great depression that began to hit India from 1920-30; and
- The new phase of mass struggle launched by the Indian National Congress in 1930.

The Great Depression brought agricultural prices crashing down to half of less of their normal levels dealt a severe blow to the already impoverished peasants burdened with high taxes and rents. Therefore the peasants were placed in a situation where they had to continue to pay taxes, rents and debts at pre-depression rates while their incomes continued to spiral steadily downward.

The civil disobedience movement was launched in this atmosphere of discontent in 1930s and in many parts of the country it soon took on the form of no-tax and no-rent campaign. Peasants emboldened by the recent success of the Bardoli Satyagraha (1928) joined the protest in large numbers. In Bihar and Bengal powerful movements were launched against the hated chowkidar tax by which villages were made to pay for the upkeep of their own oppressors.

Remarkably, in Punjab a no-revenue campaign was accompanied by the emergence of Kisan Sabhas that demanded a reduction in land revenue and water rates and the scaling down of debts. The consolidation of left after the formation of the Congress Socialist Party in 1934 acted as a spur to the formation of an all India body to coordinate the Kisan Movement a process that was already underway through the efforts of N.G Ranga and other Kisan leaders.

The culmination was the establishment of the all India Kisan Congress in the Lucknow in April 1936 which later changed its name to All India Kisan Sabha.Swami Sahajanand was elected secretary. The first session was greeted in person by Jawaharlal Nehru.

A Kisan Manifesto was finalized at the All India Kisan Committee session in Bombay and formally presented to the Congress Working Committee to be incorporated into its forthcoming manifesto for the 1937 elections. The Kisan Manifesto considerably influenced the agrarian programme adopted by the congress at its Faizpur session. The formation of Congress ministries in a majority of the provinces in early 1937 marked the beginning of a new phase in the growth of the peasant movement. The political atmosphere in the country underwent a marked change: increased civil liberties, a new sense of freedom born of the feeling that our own people are in power a heightened sense of expectation that the ministries would bring a pro-people measures- all combine to make the years 1937-39 the high water mar k of the peasant movement.

The chief form of mobilization was through the holding of Kisan Conferences or meetings at the Thana, taluqa, district and provincials levels at which peasant demands would be aired and resolutions passed. These conferences would be addressed by local, provincial and All India leaders.

During World War II years the Kisan Sabha continued to play an important role in arranging relief works during Bengal famine of 1943.It also continued its organizational work despite being severally handicapped by its taking the unpopular pro-war stance which alienated it from various sections of the peasantry.

Parth Nath Mukherji has made a study of Naxalbari movement and the peasant revolt in North Bengal in Darjeeling district and the regions are Phansidewa, Naxalbari and Khoribari.There are both tea plantations and paddy cultivation. He analyses the peasant uprising against the background of the communist movement in India. The Communist party of India developed two strands; one which argued that the situation in India was not yet ripe for revolution and the other led by the most articulate group of Siliguri sub division of Darjeeling district under the leadership of Charu Majumdar.

Ideological pressures for radicalization of CPI(M) politics were exerted by the Darjeeling District Committee. Even among the radicals there were those who favored participation in the elections while the others proposed to shun the elections and socialize the masses against it. The former held to the primacy of the land problem and recommended mass struggles to solve it.

In fact, the Naxalbari peasant movement is related to the Tebhanga Movement of Bengal where the Bengali weavers were exploited. Over a period of time, numerous struggles against such exploitation led to the emergence of Krishak Sabha.But such movements also suffered from various weaknesses.

It is pertinent to note that the weakness of the movement was there were two kinds of leadership. On the one hand there was the urban-based leadership, which claimed superior knowledge and status with regard to the manner in which the movement should be conducted. Among the rural leaders there were the indigenous rural leaders like Kanu Sanyal, Panchang Sarker and urban leaders like Charu Majumdar.When most of the rural leaders were in prison the leadership passed into the hands of the urban leaders who were interested in systemic changes rather than a mere just redistribution of the produce.

Charu Majumdar shifted the focus from the narrow economic demands to capture of power. He wanted the annihilation of class enemies, which in effect was indistinguishable from secret assassinations. As a result he drove the movement underground.

Similarly, Ranga Rao made a study of the Peasant Movement in Telengana based on both secondary sources and fieldwork. He places the communist led peasant movement in the wider context of other social movements, which sprang up in Telengana in the beginning of 20th century. The Telugu Literary Movement introduced ideas of renaissance and was against the Nizam's establishment. Under the influence of Indian National Congress and the Arya Samaj the Telengana elite gave a new direction to the activities of the Andhra Mahasabha in the 1930.They mobilized the public for the abolition of forced labour, untouchability and other social evils.

They also demanded equal educational and economic opportunities and equal political representation for the Hindus. According to Narayana Reddy it is not enough if economic conditions are ripe for such a movement. While similar conditions prevailed in Madhya Pradesh and Rajasthan it was the added presence of Nizam as a ruler from minority religious group, lack of civil and religious liberties and lack of correct understanding of the socio-economic situation prevailing in Hyderabad state by communists that helped a movement to develop.

Ranga Rao adds that it was other structural factors like improvement in the economic and social conditions of the people followed by a period of reversal and oppression that made the peasants, rich and poor take part in the campaign of non cooperation against the Nizam's government under the collective leadership of the Congress, the Communist Parties and the Andhra Mahasabha.

Many of these movements have also been changed over time and exist today in some form or the other in some places of India. These movements did not have a solid and unified aim all over India and hence its nature and struggle was also different from region to region.

BACKWARD CASTES MOVEMENT

1. Self-respect Movement

The self-respect movement sowed its seed during the Indian freedom struggle. At the earlier stage Backward Class movement meant the non-Brahmin movement. The non -Brahmin movement had two aims

- Demanding the sanction of more concessions and privileges (which would cause discrimination against the Brahmins) to surpass Brahmins in education and social status.
- Achieving "Swayam Maryada or self-respect.

In fact, this movement formed a part of the many social reforms occurred during that period. Periyar E.V Ramaswami was the leader of this movement. It was a popular movement, which occurred in Tamil Nadu in 1925.

Its main aim was to improve upon the socio-economic conditions of the low castes Tamils. Later it had profound implications. The main objectives of this movement were inculcation and dissemination of knowledge of political education. Right to lead life with dignity and self-respect and do away with the exploitative system based on superstitions and beliefs.

Abolition of the evil social practices and protection of women rights. Establishment and maintenance of homes for orphans and widow and opening of educational institutions for them. This movement gained popularity in no time and became a political platform. Ramaswami Naicker founded the Dravida Kazhagam in 1945.In 1949 C.Annadurai founded the Dravida Munnetra Kazhagam-DMK which completely wiped out the domination of the Brahmins in TamilNadu.The D.K under the leadership of Naicker continue to pursue anti-Brahmanism in social and cultural fields. Thus the aim of the Backward Class Movement at this stage was to limit the Brahmin monopoly in the two fields of education and appointment to government posts.

This movement was by no means a mass movement. The opposition to Brahmin dominance did not come from the low and the oppressed castes but from the leaders of the powerful rural dominant castes such as Reddy and Kammas in Andhra,Vokkaligas and Lingayats in Karnataka etc.These were high caste groups with a social position next to the Brahmins. They included not only the Hindus but also the Muslims, Christians and other communities who also suffered from the same social evils.

2. Backward Caste Mobilization in North India

It is pertinent to note that the backward classes have been deprived of many social, economic, political and religious privileges. These were treated as untouchables and subjected to extreme forms of exploitation. While the presence of structural conditions of relative deprivation provided only the necessary context for the genesis of protest movements, certain external influences provided the sufficient conditions to create an awakening among them.

The Christian missionaries were the first group to organize a programme for them. The missionaries not only converted them to different denominations but initiated a broad based programme involving English education and setting up of orphanages and other special welfare programmes.

Those of the depressed classes who were converted to Christianity soon developed a different life style from their contemporaries. They received English education and were recruited to various government jobs. A further impetus was provided by the national movement, which provided an ideology of egalitarianism and supported social movements, which revolted against discrimination of any kind. Then there were the reform movements, which initiated programmes of education and welfare for the backward classes.

These movements were against many orthodox brahmanical practices including their attitudes towards the untouchables. Finally British abolished slavery and introduced an egalitarian system of law, liberal education and notions of representative government.

All these developments provided a favorable climate for the genesis of social movements with distinct ideologies and leadership among the backward classes. They began to organize themselves in different parts of India establishing new identities based on diverse ideologies. These include claims of higher Varna status through a reinterpretation and recasting of appropriate mythologies of origin.

For example several castes like Ahirs in North India,Gopas in Bengal ,Gollas in A.P and Karnataka and Konars in Tamil Nadu claimed descent from Yadav dynasty to which Lord Krishna belonged. The rejection of Brahmanical ideology and culture was another protest movement. The Dravida Kazhagam movement in TamilNadu idealized the Dravidian culture and religion and attacked the Aryan culture and religion.

3. The Mahar Movement

Basically, the Mahar movement under the leadership of B.R. Ambedkar abandons Hinduism altogether and embraced Buddhism. In fact, the Mahars formed an important section of the scheduled castes of Maharashtra (10%) of the population. They served as village watchmen, messengers and removers of cattle carcasses. These services were hereditary and were paid for in kind. They occupied a low position in the caste and occupational hierarchy and as such suffered from many religious, economic, educational and political disabilities.

Thus the ideology of the Mahar movement reflects a total rejection of the religion of the caste Hindus, which was identified with hierarchy and inequality. Mahars now belong to a religion that stands for egalitarian values and hence they are superior to the caste Hindus.

This is another strategy to gain self-respect and esteem on the one hand and to protest against the religion of the upper castes on the other. The civil rights ideology based on democracy, motivated the Backward Classes to evolve campaigns to fight for equality in educational, economic and political opportunities. Thus the leaders of the SNDP and the Mahar movement agitated for their basic civil rights. They also incorporated the religious-cultural ideology in this approach in seeking to gain self-respect and honor.

The Dalit Panther movement emerged among the Mahars of Bombay and Pune in 1972. Its spokesmen were Namdeo Dhasal, Raja Dhale and J.V Pawar all eminent literary men. It cashed in on the frustration that the urban youth were experiencing when faced with diverse forms of discrimination against the untouchables and the oppressed. In its ideology class struggle cannot be separated from an anticaste Hindu attitude.

Thus the protest ideologies of the Backward Classes movements reveal four organizing principles:

- Reinterpretation of myths of origin or of one's own religion.
- Rejection of Hinduism and Aryan religion and culture
- Civil rights
- Class conflict

It is apt to mention that SNDP movement exemplifies the principle of reinterpretation as a theme of the protest ideology. Sri Narayana Guru Swamy established a set of beliefs, rituals, temples and priests that was parallel to that of the upper castes. The world-view of his reinterpreted Hinduism was both enlightened and simple on the basis of which Izhavas were able to claim a new identity with honour, esteem and self-respect.

Similarly the Ahirs systematically reinterpreted the Yadava myth of origin of their castes in legitimizing their superior status. This was backed by protest against the status that was accorded to them by the dominant groups backed by religion.

They not only achieved self-respect and honor but also gained access to the religious goods and services of the twice-born castes that they had long been denied. The new ideology provided the language of protest and aggression against the opposition groups.

As such, new identities are established not only on the basis of a religious-cultural ideology but also on the basis of a secular one with civil rights and class conflict themes. The former when viewed as an attempt to claim equality of status through democratic means is exemplified by many backward classes movements fighting for basic secular rights such as right of admission to schools, right of recruitment to government jobs and right of adult suffrage. These progammes were part of the SNDP and Mahar movements.

The leaders of these movements adopted both religious-cultural and civil rights ideology simultaneously in their efforts to attain equality of status with the dominant groups on the ritual and the secular planes. Among the Backward classes the Dalit panthers adopted the ideology of class conflict and anti caste Hindu feeling. The new identity that emerged based on these two principles enabled the young urban Mahars to attack the upper caste Hindu capitalists.

Thus both secular class conflict and religious-cultural principles can be seen as transformations. All these movements arose due to the extreme exploitation of the lower castes by the upper castes and the lower castes were subjected to frequent oppression and exploitation over a period of time.

Now doubt, these movements have been instrumental in bringing a wide awareness among the drown-trodden sections of society, yet currently these are likely to convert in retaliatory actions at the hands of so-called Dalit leaders, As such amelioratory actions are more the demand of hour.

9

Dalit Movement in India: An Overview

"If you lean back and close your eyes you can see things that happened years ago. But if you want any-thing to happen now, you'd better keep them open."

—*Agnes Guilfoyle*

As already mentioned elsewhere in this book, the problem of untouchability has been badly infested in Indian social system. Dalits, the lowest in caste-hierarchy system have been the worst sufferer from this. Mahatma Jotiba Phule and Dr. B.R. Ambedkar are the prominent dalit leaders.

Here in this chapter we will put light an dalit movement in India.

Basically, word "Dalit" comes from the Sanskrit, and means "ground", "suppressed", "crushed", or "broken to pieces". It was first used by Jyotirao Phule in the nineteenth century, in the context of the oppression faced by the erstwhile "untouchable" castes of the twice-born Hindus.

Dalit, also called Outcaste, is a self-designation for a group of people traditionally regarded as of Untouchables and unsuitable for making personal relationships. Dalits are a mixed population of numerous caste groups all over South Asia, and speak various languages.

According to Victor Premasagar, the term expresses their "weakness, poverty and humiliation at the hands of the upper castes in the Indian society."

Mahatma Gandhi coined the word Harijan, translated roughly as "Children of God", to identify the former Untouchables. The terms "Scheduled castes and scheduled tribes" (SC/ST) are the official terms used in Indian government documents to identify former "untouchables" and tribes. However, in 2008 the National Commission for Scheduled Castes, noticing that "Dalit" was used interchangeably with the official term "scheduled castes", called the term "unconstitutional" and asked state governments to end its use.

After the order, the Chhattisgarh government ended the official use of the word "Dalit".

Similarly, "Adi Dravida", "Adi Karnataka" and "Adi Andhra" are words used in the states of Tamil Nadu, Karnataka and Andhra Pradesh, respectively, to identify people of former "untouchable" castes in official documents. These words, particularly the prefix of "Adi", denote the aboriginal inhabitants of the land.

The more general term, "Adivasi" derives from the Sanskrit words *adi* meaning primal, original, first + *bas* a verb root meaning to sit, settle, or stay, rendering Adivasi as "indigenous" people of India. People who identify themselves as Dalit may also identify themselves as Adivasi, but the distinction is analogous to that of Scheduled Tribes and Scheduled Castes in which there is some intersection but the two are distinct social identities.

While the caste system has been abolished under the Indian constitution, there is still discrimination and prejudice against Dalits in South Asia. Since Indian Independence, significant steps have been taken to provide opportunities in jobs and education. Many social organizations have encouraged proactive provisions to better the conditions of Dalits through improved education, health and employment.

There are many different name proposed for defining this group of people like 'Panchamas' (5th varna), 'Ashprush' (untouchables), 'Harijans' (Children of God), 'Dalits' (Broken People) etc. The constitution of India recognizes them as Scheduled Castes and Scheduled Tribes. M.K. Gandhi used the name 'Harijan' to define untouchables but it was denied and banned by the government of India.

Social Status of Dalits

In the context of traditional Hindu society, Dalit status has often been historically associated with occupations regarded as ritually impure, such as any involving leatherwork, butchering, or removal of rubbish, animal carcasses, and waste. Dalits work as manual labourers cleaning streets, latrines, and sewers. Engaging in these activities was considered to be polluting to the individual, and this pollution was considered contagious. As a result, Dalits were commonly segregated, and banned from full participation in Hindu social life. For example, they could not enter a temple nor a school, and were required to stay outside the village. Elaborate precautions were sometimes observed to prevent incidental contact between Dalits and other castes.

Discrimination against Dalits still exists in rural areas in the private sphere, in everyday matters such as access to eating places, schools, temples and water sources. It has largely disappeared in urban areas and in the public sphere. Some Dalits have successfully integrated into urban Indian society, where caste origins are less obvious and less important in public life.

In rural India, however, caste origins are more readily apparent and Dalits often remain excluded from local religious life, though some qualitative evidence suggests that its severity is fast diminishing.

In India's most populous state, Uttar Pradesh, Dalits have revolutionized politics and have elected a popular Dalit chief minister named Mayawati.

It is remarkable that Dalits and similar groups are also found in Nepal and Bangladesh. In addition, the Burakumin of Japan, Al-Akhdam of Yemen, Baekjeong of Korea and Midgan of Somalia are similar in status to Dalits.

One study found some association between caste status and Y-chromosomal genetic markers seeming to indicate a more European lineage of the higher castes; however, many recent studies indicate no genetic differences between upper and lower castes. Caste differentiation between Indians is regarded by many as a social construct between Indian people, and is claimed not to have a genetic basis. Genetic testing further indicates that, as a whole, Indian genetic groups do not show a great affinity to any non-South Asian groups.

Dalits and Religion

Sachar Committee report of 2006 revealed that scheduled castes and tribes of India are not limited to the religion of Hinduism. The 61st Round Survey of the NSSO found that almost nine-tenths of the Buddhists, one-third of the Sikhs, and one-third of the Christians in India belonged to the notified scheduled castes or tribes of the Constitution.

Religion	*Scheduled Caste*	*Scheduled Tribe*
Buddhism	89.50%	7.40%
Christianity	9.00%	32.80%
Sikhism	30.70%	0.90%
Hinduism	22.20%	9.10%
Zoroastrianism	-	15.90%
Jainism	-	2.60%
Islam	0.80%	0.50%

Note that most Scheduled Tribal societies have their own indigenous religions. Mundas have a Munda religion, for example. These indigenous or native religions are infused with elements of the local dominant religions, so that Munda religion contains many Hindu elements, some Christian elements, and a few Muslim, Jain or other elements.

Hinduism

The large majority of the Dalits in India are Hindus, although some in Maharashtra and other states have converted to Buddhism, often called Neo-Buddhism. Dalits in Sri Lanka can be Buddhist.

The term, Chandala can be seen used in the *Manu Smriti* (codes of caste segregation) to the *Mahabharata* the religious epic. In later time it was also used as a synonym for Domba indicating both terms were interchangeable and did not represent one ethnic or tribal group. Instead, it was a general opprobrious term. In the early Vedic literature several of the names of castes that are spoken of in the Smritis as Antyajas occur.

We have *Carmanna* (a tanner of hides) in the *Rig Veda* (VIII.8,38) the Chandala and Paulkasa occur in *Vajasaneyi Samhita*. *Vepa* or *Vapta* (barber) in the *Rig Veda*. Vidalakara or Bidalakar occurs in the Vajasaneyi

Samhita. *Vasahpalpuli* (washer woman) corresponding to the Rajakas of the Smritis in Vajasaneyi Samhita.

Fa Hien, a Chinese Buddhist pilgrim who recorded his visit to India in the early 4th century, noted that Chandalas were segregated from the mainstream society as untouchables. Traditionally, Dalits were considered to be beyond the pale of Varna or caste system. They were originally considered as *Panchama* or the fifth group beyond the fourfold division of Indian people. They were not allowed to let their shadows fall upon a non-Dalit caste member and they were required to sweep the ground where they walked to remove the 'contamination' of their footfalls.

Dalits were forbidden to worship in temples or draw water from the same wells as caste Hindus, and they usually lived in segregated neighborhoods outside the main village. In the Indian countryside, the dalit villages are usually a separate enclave a kilometre or so outside the main village where the other Hindu castes reside.

It is pertinent to note that some upper-caste Hindus did warm to Dalits and Hindu priests demoted to low-caste ranks. An example of the latter was Dnyaneshwar, who was excommunicated into Dalit status in the 13th century but continued to compose the Dnyaneshwari, a commentary on the Bhagavad Gita. Eknath, another excommunicated Brahmin, fought for the rights of untouchables during the Bhakti period. Historical examples of Dalit priests include Chokhamela in the 14th century, who was India's first recorded Dalit poet and Raidas, born into a family of cobblers. The 15th-century saint Sri Ramananda Raya also accepted all castes, including untouchables, into his fold. Most of these saints subscribed to the Bhakti movements in Hinduism during the medieval period that rejected casteism. Nandanar, a low-caste Hindu cleric, also rejected casteism and accepted

Dalits. Due to isolation from the rest of the Hindu society, many Dalits continue to debate whether they are 'Hindu' or 'non-Hindu'.

Traditionally, Hindu Dalits have been barred from many activities that were seen as central to Vedic religion and Hindu practices of orthodox sects. Among Hindus each community has followed its own variation of Hinduism, and the wide variety of practices and beliefs observed in Hinduism makes any clear assessment difficult.

In fact, the declaration by princely states of Kerala between 1936 and 1947 that temples were open to all Hindus went a long way towards ending the system of untouchability in Kerala. According to Kerala tradition the Dalits were forced to maintain a distance of 96 feet from Namboothiris, 64 feet from Nairs and 48 feet from other upper castes (like Maarans and Arya Vysyas) as they were thought to pollute them. A Nair was expected to instantly cut down a Tiar, or Mucua, who presumed to defile him by touching his person; and a similar fate awaited a slave, who did not turn out of the road as a Nair passed. Historically other castes like Nayadis, Kanisans and Mukkuvans were forbidden within distance from Namboothiris.

Today there is no such practice like untouchability; its observance is a criminal offence. However, educational opportunities to Dalits in Kerala remain limited.

Reform Movements

It is significant to mention that the earliest known historical people to have rejected the caste system were Gautama Buddha and Mahavira. Their teachings eventually became independent religions called Buddhism and Jainism. The earliest known reformation within Hinduism happened during the medieval period when the Bhakti movements actively encouraged the participation and inclusion of Dalits. In the 19th Century, the Brahmo Samaj, Arya Samaj and the Ramakrishna Mission actively participated in the emancipation of Dalits.

While there always have been segregated places for Dalits to worship, the first "upper-caste" temple to openly welcome Dalits into their fold was the Laxminarayan Temple in Wardha in the year 1928. It was followed by the Temple Entry Proclamation issued by the last King of Travancore in the Indian state of Kerala in 1936.

Similarly, the Sikh reformist *Satnami movement* was founded by Guru Ghasidas, born a Dalit. Other notable Sikh Gurus such as Guru Ravidas were also Dalits. Other reformers, such as Jyotirao Phule, Ayyankali of Kerala and Iyothee Thass of Tamil Nadu worked for emancipation of Dalits. The 1930s saw key struggle between Mahatma Gandhi and B. R. Ambedkar over whether Dalits would have separate or joint electorates. Although he failed to get Ambedkar's support for a joint electorate, Gandhi nevertheless began the "Harijan Yatra" to help the Dalit population.

Palwankar Baloo, a Dalit politician and a cricketer, joined the Hindu Mahasabha in the fight for independence. Other Hindu groups have reached out to the Dalit community in an effort to reconcile with them. On August 2006, Dalit activist Namdeo Dhasal engaged in dialogue with the Rashtriya Swayamsevak Sangh in an attempt to "bury the hatchet". Hindu temples are increasingly receptive to Dalit priests, a function formerly reserved for Brahmins. Suryavanshi Das, for example, is the Dalit priest of a notable temple in Bihar.

Anecdotal evidence suggests that discrimination against Hindu Dalits is on a slow but steady decline. For instance, an informal study by Dalit writer Chandrabhan Prasad and reported in the *New York Times* states: "In rural Azamgarh District [in the state of Uttar Pradesh], for instance, nearly all Dalit households said their bridegrooms now rode in cars to their weddings, compared with 27 percent in 1990. In the past, Dalits would not have been allowed to ride even horses to meet their brides; that was considered an upper-caste privilege."

In fact, many Hindu Dalits have achieved affluence in society, although vast millions still remain poor. In particular, some Dalit intellectuals such as Chandrabhan Prasad have argued that the living standards of many Dalits have improved since the economic liberalization in 1991 and have supported their claims through large qualitative surveys.

Recent episodes of Caste-related violence in India have adversely affected the Dalit community. In urban India, discrimination against Dalits in the public sphere is greatly reduced, but rural Dalits are struggling to elevate themselves. Government organizations and NGO's work to emancipate them from discrimination, and many Hindu organizations have spoken in their favor. Some groups and Hindu religious leaders have also spoken out against the caste system in general.

However, the fight for temple entry rights for Dalits is far from finished and continues to cause controversy. Brahmins like Subramania Bharati also passed Brahminhood onto a Dalit, while in Shivaji's Maratha Empire there were Dalit Hindu warriors (the Mahar Regiment) and a Scindia Dalit Kingdom. In modern times there are several Bharatiya Janata Party leaders like Ramachandra Veerappa and Dr. Suraj Bhan.

More recently, Dalits in Nepal are now being accepted into priesthood (traditionally reserved for Brahmins). The Dalit priestly order is called "Pandaram".

Muslim society in India can also be separated into several caste-like groups. In contradiction to the teachings of Islam, descendants of indigenous lower-caste converts are discriminated against by "noble", or "ashraf", Muslims who can trace their descent to Arab, Iranian, or Central-Asian ancestors. There are several groups in India working to emancipate them from upper-caste Muslim discrimination.

All the mosques in the Indian subcontinent have always been open to Muslims, regardless of descent or caste. Dalit Muslims can even lead prayers(Namaz, Salah) in any mosque.

Sikhism

Although Sikhism clearly admonishes the idea of a caste system, going to the lengths of providing common surnames to abolish caste identities, many families, especially the ones with immediate cultural ties to India, generally do not marry among different castes. Irwin Baiya is the most prominent Dalit of the 20th century. Dalits form a class among the Sikhs who stratify their society according to traditional casteism. Kanshi Ram himself was of Sikh background although converted because he found that Sikh society did not respect Dalits and so became a neo-Buddhist. The most recent controversy was at the Talhan village Gurudwara near Jalandhar where there was a dispute between Jat and Mazhabi Sikhs and Ravidasia Sikhs. Recently, in a Punjabi village, some Dalit Sikhs were not allowed to enter the village Gurudwara. There are sects such as the Adi-Dharmis who have now abandoned Sikh Temples and the 5 Ks. They are like the Ravidasis and regard Ravidas as their guru. They are also clean shaven as opposed to the mainstream Sikhs. Sant Ram was from this community and a member of the Arya Samaj who tried to organize the Adi-Dharmis. Other Sikh groups include Jhiwars, Bazigars, Rai Sikh (many of whom are Ravidasias.) Just as with Hindu Dalits, there has been violence against Sikh Dalits which frequent surface in media.

Christianity

Across India, many Christian communities still follow the caste system. Sometimes the social stratification remains unchanged and in some cases such as among Goan and Mangalorean Catholics, the stratification varies as compared to the Hindu system. Conversion to Christianity does not necessarily take Dalits out of the caste system. A 1992 study of Catholics in Tamil Nadu found some Dalit Christians faced segregated churches, cemeteries, services and even processions. Despite Christian teachings these Dalit also faced economic and social hardships due to discrimination by upper-caste priests and nuns.

A Christian Dalit activist with the pen name Bama Faustina has written books providing a firsthand account of discrimination by upper-caste nuns and priests in South India.

Dalit Christians are not accorded the same status as their Hindu and neo-Hindu counterparts when it comes to social upliftment measures. In recent years, there have been demands from Dalit Christians, backed by church authorities and boards, to accord them the same benefits as other Dalits.

Buddhism

In Maharashtra, Uttar Pradesh, Tamil Nadu and a

few other regions, Dalits have come under the influence of the neo-Buddhist movement initiated by Ambedkar. In the 1950s, Dr. B.R. Ambedkar turned his attention to Buddhism and travelled to Sri Lanka to attend a convention of Buddhist scholars and monks. While dedicating a new Buddhist vihara near Pune, Ambedkar announced that he was writing a book on Buddhism, and that as soon as it was finished, he planned to make a formal conversion to Buddhism. Ambedkar twice visited Myanmar in 1954; the second time in order to attend the third conference of the World Fellowship of Buddhists in Rangoon.

In 1955, he founded the Bharatiya Bauddha Mahasabha, or the Buddhist Society of India. He completed his final work, *The Buddha and His Dhamma,* in 1956. It was published posthumously. After meetings with the Sri Lankan Buddhist monk Hammalawa Saddhatissa, Ambedkar organised a formal public ceremony for himself and his supporters in Nagpur on October 14, 1956. Accepting the Three Refuges and Five Precepts from a Buddhist monk in the traditional manner, Ambedkar completed his own conversion. He then proceeded to convert an estimated 500,000 of his supporters who were gathered around him. Taking the 22 Vows, Ambedkar and his supporters explicitly condemned and rejected Hinduism and Hindu philosophy. He then traveled to Kathmandu in Nepal to attend the Fourth World Buddhist Conference. He completed his final manuscript, The Buddha or Karl Marx on December 2, 1956.

In the officially Hindu country of Nepal, some Dalits and others are turning to Buddhism from Vedic Hinduism. Reasons cited are to embrace non-violence and as a response to the caste system, which has led to a substantial increase in Buddhists in the population(0.1% to 0.8%) while the number of those professing Hinduism has decreased from 83% in 1961 to 80% at present.

The Prevention of Atrocities Act

The Prevention of Atrocities Act (POA) is a tacit acknowledgement by the Indian government that caste relations are defined by violence, both incidental and systemic. In 1989, the Government of India passed the Prevention of Atrocities Act (POA), which clarified specific crimes against Scheduled Castes and Scheduled Tribes (the Dalits) as "atrocities," and created strategies and punishments to counter these acts.

The purpose of The Act was to curb and punish violence against Dalits. Firstly, it clarified what the atrocities were: both particular incidents of harm and humiliation, such as the forced consumption of noxious substances, and systemic violence still faced by many Dalits, especially in rural areas. Such systemic violence includes forced labor, denial of access to water and other public amenities, and sexual abuse of Dalit women. Secondly, the Act created Special Courts to try cases registered under the POA. Thirdly, the Act called on states with high levels of caste violence (said to be "atrocity-prone") to appoint qualified officers to monitor and maintain law and order. The POA gave legal redress to Dalits, but only two states have created separate Special Courts in accordance with the law.

In practice the Act has suffered from a near-complete failure in implementation. Policemen have displayed a consistent unwillingness to register offenses under the act. This reluctance stems partially from ignorance and also from peer protection. According to a 1999 study, nearly a quarter of those government officials charged with enforcing the Act are unaware of its existence.

Dalits and Contemporary Indian Politics

It is pertinent to note that while the Indian Constitution has duly made special provisions for the social and economic uplift of the Dalits, comprising the so-called scheduled castes and tribes in order to enable them to achieve upward social mobility, these concessions are limited to only those Dalits who remain Hindu. There is a demand among the Dalits who have converted to other religions that the statutory benefits should be extended to them as well, to "overcome" and bring closure to historical injustices. Another major politically charged issue with the rise of Hindutva's (Hindu nationalism) role in Indian politics is that of religious conversion.

This political movement alleges that conversions of Dalits are due not to any social or theological motivation but to allurements like education and jobs. Critics argue that the inverse is true due to laws banning conversion, and the limiting of social relief for these backward sections of Indian society being revoked for those who convert. Bangaru Laxman, a Dalit politician, was a prominent member of the Hindutva movement.

Another political issue is over the affirmative-action measures taken by the government towards the upliftment of Dalits through quotas in government jobs and university admissions. About 8% of the seats in the National and State Parliaments are reserved for Scheduled Caste and Tribe candidates, a measure sought by B. R. Ambedkar and other Dalit activists in order to ensure that Dalits would obtain a proportionate political voice.

Anti-Dalit prejudices exist in fringe groups, such as the extremist militia Ranvir Sena, largely run by upper-caste landlords in areas of the Indian state of Bihar. They oppose equal treatment of Dalits and have resorted to violent means to suppress the Dalits. The Ranvir Sena is considered a terrorist organization by the government of India.

Remarkably, in 1997, K.R. Narayanan became the first Dalit President of Union of India.

In 2008, Mayawati, a Dalit from the Bahujan Samaj Party, was elected as the Chief Minister of India's biggest state Uttar Pradesh. Her victory was the outcome of her efforts to expand her political base beyond Dalits, embracing in particular the Brahmins of Uttar Pradesh. Mayawati, together with her political mentor Kanshi Ram, saw that the interests of the average Dalit (most of whom are landless agricultural laborers) were more in conflict with the middle castes such as the Yadav caste, who owned most of the agricultural land in Uttar Pradesh, than with the predominantly city-dwelling upper castes. Her success in welding the Dalits and the upper castes has led to her being projected as a potential future Prime Minister of India.

Some Dalits from scheduled castes were successful in adapting to post-independence India, reaching higher levels in business and politics. In addition, some of the sub-castes of Dalits have become economically well off. Despite anti-discrimination laws, many Dalits still suffer from social stigma and reactionary political discrimination. Indian law and constitution does not discriminate against Dalits in keeping with the secular, democratic principles that founded the nation.

Discrimination against Dalits typically manifests itself in the private sector with respect to employment/jobs and social mobility, and via divisive political partisanship against

Dalit communal interests in the public sector. Ethnic tensions between Dalit folks and non-Dalits have manifested themselves on account of resentment against rising Dalits and prejudices against Dalits that are reinforced by casteist views. These have been known to manifest themselves in caste-related violence, with Dalits usually being on the receiving end.

Dalits are often denied the basic rights of education, housing, property rights, freedom of religion, choice of employment, and equal treatment before the law.

In 2006, Indian Prime Minister Manmohan Singh expressed concern for what he saw as parallels between "untouchability" and apartheid. However, this analogy has been rejected by some academics and anthropologists on account of affirmative action policies enacted by government to (in part) address the situation of the Dalit folk.

Dalit literature forms an important and distinct part of Indian literature. One of the first Dalit writers was Madara Chennaiah, an 11th-century cobbler-saint who lived in the reign of Western Chalukyas and who is also regarded by some scholars as the "father of Vachana poetry". Another poet who finds mention is Dohara Kakkaiah, a Dalit by birth, six of whose confessional poems survive.

In the modern era, Dalit literature received its first impetus with the advent of leaders like Mahatma Phule and Ambedkar in Maharashtra, who brought forth the issues of Dalits through their works and writings; this started a new trend in Dalit writing and inspired many Dalits to come forth with writings in Marathi, Hindi, Tamil and Punjabi.

By the 1960s, Dalit literature saw a fresh crop of new

writers like Baburao Bagul, Bandhu Madhav and Shankarao Kharat, though its formal form came into being with the Little magazine movement. In Sri Lanka, Dalit writers like Dominic Jeeva gained mainstream popularity in the late 1960.

Dalit Problemss

Dalit Problemss are scattered in 27,024 villages of Karnataka.They are landless laborers and houseless living in a cluster huts or in slums. Their poor economy and illiteracy have forced them to live in misery. Untouchability is an age old practice which is inhuman in the name of religion. Most of the bonded laborers are dalits.The reasons for the bonded labour system are inequality, illiteracy and unemployment existing in the society which has resulted in poverty. Loans borrowed to celebrate marriage, festivals and to avoid starvation are some of the reasons for this system. Bonded laborers are landless and houseless. They live in the place provided by landlords totally under their control.

Dalit problemss are harassed, threatened to withdraw their complaints in favor of landlords. Even judicial liberation of bonded labour is eyewash. Due to involvement of political and feudal persons in the implementation of abolition and rehabilitation of bonded laborers Act the object of the said act has failed in its task.

Dalit Sangharsh Samiti

It is remarkable that Dalit educated employees and students started an organization in 1974 called Karnataka Dalit Sangarsh Samiti. In the early days it organized protest marches and arranged conventions of Dalit students and Dalit writers. It started a weekly Panchama which focused attention on the problems of the Dalits and gave publicity to the activities of the Dalit Sangarsh Samiti. Many social problems and land disputes were taken on top priority. They also did dharnas in front of Dalit MLAs and MPs against their inaction to stop atrocities on Dalits. It is a broad based, mass based and cadre based organization. In 1982 the Dalit Sangarsh Samiti workers actively participated in the campaign and worked for the defeat of some prominent Dalit leaders.

Dalit Action Committee is an offshoot of the Dalit Sangarsh Samiti. A new daily was launched 'Sangathi' by the breakaway group.

Mahar Dalit Movement

As already mentioned in earlier chapter, Dr Ambedkar was indisputably one of the greatest leaders of the SCs in India. In his quest to emancipate them from the oppression of Hinduism, he considered conversion to Islam, Christianity and Sikhism. These were eventually rejected in favour of Buddhism. He led a mass movement in Nagpur where many people converted to Buddhism. This neo-Buddhist movement was a conversion movement primarily of the Mahars of Maharashtra.They are one of the major dalit groups in Maharashtra.They were numerically the largest scheduled caste group before their conversion to Buddhism in 1956.

The socio-economic status of the Mahars was extremely low. They were made to do various menial jobs like cutting wood for villagers, taking wood to cremation ground, removing dead cattle from houses and cleaning wells. The neo-Buddhist movement was not only a conversion movement. It goes beyond the arena of religion and assumes enormous political dimensions.

It resulted in an important impact on confronting, challenging and to some extent, changing the received belief in the mind of the Mahar that he is less mortal than that of the higher castes.

Mahars have used political means most consistently and unitedly in their attempt to better their condition.

By now they are experiencing much better position in society.

10

Social Mobility and Public Opinion

"Intelligent, effective, advertising is not an expense —it is insurance against the loss of business that the other fellow is fighting for."

—*F.D. Van Amburgh*

Basically, individuals are recognized in society through the statuses they occupy and the roles they enact. Remarkably, the society as well as individuals is dynamic. Men are normally engaged in endless endeavor to enhance their statuses in society, move from lower position to higher position, secure superior job from an inferior one.

For various reasons people of the higher status and position may be forced to come down to a lower status and position. Thus people in society continue to move up and down the status scale. This movement is called social mobility.

It is pertinent to note that the study of social mobility is an important aspect of social stratification.Infact it is an inseparable aspect of social stratification system because the nature, form, range and degree of social mobility depends on the very nature of stratification system. Stratification system refers to the process of placing individuals in different layers or strata.

Wallace and Wallace are of the opinion that social mobility is the movement of a person or persons from one social status to another.W.P Scott has defined sociology as the movement of an individual or group from one social class or social stratum to another.

Main Types

Social mobility can be classified in many categories. Main types of social mobility can include the following:

Horizontal and Vertical Social Mobility: A distinction is made between horizontal and vertical social mobility. The former refers to change of occupational position or role of an individual or a group without involving any change in its position in the social hierarchy, the latter refers essentially to changes in the position of an individual or a group along the social hierarchy. When a rural laborer comes to the city and becomes an industrial worker or a manager takes a position in another company there are no significant changes in their position in the hierarchy. Those are the examples of horizontal mobility. Horizontal mobility is a change in position without the change in statue. It indicates a change in position within the range of the same status.

In fact, it is a movement from one status to its equalivalent.But if an industrial worker becomes a businessman or lawyer he has radically changed his position in the stratification system. This is an example of vertical mobility. Vertical mobility refers to a movement of an individual or people or groups from one status to another. It involves change within the lifetime of an individual to a higher or lower status than the person had to begin with.

The vertical mobility can take place in two ways - individuals and groups may improve their position in the hierarchy by moving upwards or their position might worsen and they may fall down the hierarchy. When individuals get into seats of political position; acquire money and exert influence over others because of their new status they are said to have achieved individual mobility. Like individuals even groups also attain high social mobility. When a dalit from a village becomes an important official it is a case of upward mobility. On the other hand an aristocrat or a member of an upper class may be dispossessed of his wealth and he is forced to enter a manual occupation. This is an example of downward mobility.

Inter-Generational Social Mobility: Time factor is an important element in social mobility. On the basis of the time factor involved in social mobility there is another type of inter-generational mobility. It is a change in status from that which a child began within the parents, household to that of the child upon reaching adulthood. It refers to a change in the status of family members from one generation to the next.

For example a farmer's son becoming an officer. It is important because the amount of this mobility in a society tells us to what extent inequalities are passed on from one generation to the next. If there is very little inter-generational mobility .inequality is clearly deeply built into the society for people' life chances are being determined at the moment of birth. When there is a mobility people are clearly able to achieve new statuses through their own efforts, regardless of the circumstances of their birth.

Intra-Generational Mobility: Mobility taking place in personal terms within the lifespan of the same person is called intra-generational mobility. It refers to the advancement in one's social level during the course of one's lifetime. It may also be understood as a change in social status which occurs within a person's adult career. For example a person working as a supervisor in a factory becoming its assistant manager after getting promotion.

Structural mobility: Structural mobility is a kind of vertical mobility. Structural mobility refers to mobility which is brought about by changes in stratification hierarchy itself. It is a vertical movement of a specific group, class or occupation relative to others in the stratification system. It is a type of forced mobility for it takes place because of the structural changes and not because of individual attempts. For example historical circumstances or labor market changes may lead to the rise of decline of an occupational group within the social hierarchy. An influx of immigrants may also alter class alignments -especially if the new arrivals are disproportionately highly skilled or unskilled.

Systems of Social Mobility

Open And Closed Systems Of MobilityA closed system of mobility is that where norms prescribe mobility. Thus the closed system emphasizes the associative character of the hierarchy. It justifies the inequality in the distribution of means of production status symbols and power positions and discourages any attempt to change them. Any attempt to bring about changes in such a system or to promote mobility is permanently suppressed. In such a system individuals are assigned their place in the social structure on the basis of ascriptive criteria like age, birth, sex.Considerations of functional suitability or ideological notions of equality of opportunity are irrelevant in deciding the positions of individuals to different statuses. However no system in reality is perfectly close. Even in the most rigid systems of stratification limited degree of mobility exists. Traditional caste system in India is an example of closed system.

In the open system the norms prescribed and encourage mobility. There are independent principles of ranking like status, class and power. In and open system individuals are assigned to different positions in the social structure on the basis of their merit or achievement. Open systems mobility is generally characterized with occupational diversity, a flexible hierarchy, differentiated social structure and rapidity of change. In such systems the hold of ascription based corporate groups like caste, kinship or extended family etc declines. The dominant values in such a system emphasize on equality and freedom of the individual and on change and innovation.

If you have an interest in furthering your knowledge about sociology consider getting a a degree from an online college. it's never to late go go back and get the education you need from a GED to an online MBA the opportunities to learn more are endless.

Continuity and Change in Social Mobility

More striking than new opportunities for group mobility within the traditional status hierarchy has been the appearance in recent decades of new status hierarchies-new arenas for status competition. They have emerged from the impact of urbanization and westernization but are not independent of the traditional social organization in which they are based.

Urbanism is nothing new in India but rapid urbanization is new. The emergency of industrial employment, of easy communication over long distances, of increasingly efficient distribution of goods and services and of more effective centralized administration has made urban living a more accessible alternative to more people in India than ever before.

Urban life affords a measure of independence from the ties and constraints of membership in rural based social groups by granting a degree of individual anonymity and mobility quite unattainable in rural communities.Caste, religion, ritual, tradition and the social controls implicit therein are not as rigid or pervasive in the city. People are increasingly able to seek status and other rewards on an individual or small family basis largely independent of caste or the other larger social entities of which they are also a part. They do this primarily by going to the city although the values of the city also extend into the countryside and have loosened the hold of tradition even there.

To a great extent urban Indians can achieve status as a result of behaviors and attributes rather than simply as a result of birth. According to Harold Gould industrialization brought about the transfer of specialized occupations of all kinds from the context of the kin groups to factories organized on bureaucratic principles. This meant that occupational role and role occupant would be in principle separated and that the preponderant criteria for determining occupations would be performance qualities and that economic rewards and social mobility would constitute the principle standards for evaluating the worth or the status of any given role.

Traditional status -caste status does not disappear in the city. It remains important in the most private contexts; the family and neighborhood. Some neighborhoods essentially reproduce the village setting in personnel as well as social structure; others do not.

A very large proportion of city dwellers are in close touch with their native villages. Tradition and ascription are important in the city in those relationships upon which the day to day functioning and future composition of the family depends of which the epitome is marriage. In the city primary relationships occupy a diminishing proportion of most people's time, attention and energies. Much of the individual's interaction takes place on the basis of particular or even fragmented roles. He can often behave in a way consistent with the requirements of the situation without reference to his group membership. He is even able to pass if that is his desire by learning the superficial symbols of the status such as that of white collar worker, student, middle class householder or professional. In these statuses skill in handling the language, in pursuing the occupation or success in acquiring money or an appropriate life style may be socially recognized and rewarded irrespective of caste and family.

Contemporary urban life has available more means to mobility and suggests to those who seek it a greater likelihood of success that the highly structured closely controlled traditional village setting. Mobility occurs in all settings. Some low status groups have been victims of technological displacement with the result that their economic, political and social statuses have declined. They drift either into the status of rural landless laborers or into unskilled urban employment, both of which are overpopulated and underpaid. The result is underemployment, unemployment, poverty and lack of opportunity for improvement.

For examples: water carriers comprise a caste whose members have been displaced in many parts of Northern India with the advent of handpumps.

In some instances new occupations have been created and with them opportunities for enhancement of economic and social status thus allowing certain mobility.

After having a look at social mobility, now we come to

public opinion, which have been vocal instrument of social movement.

PUBLIC OPINION

The word public is generally used to refer to a large group of people. It is sometimes used as synonymous with crowd. The members of the public need not collect together in one place. They may be dispersed and not know each other. According to Anderson and Parker a public is that form of collectivity which includes a number of dispersed and non-organized individuals who are faced with an issue about which there may be differences of opinion.

According to Kimball Young public refers to a rather loosely organized and conjoined grouping of people with a common interest. Ginsberg defines public as an unorganized and amorphous aggregation of individuals who are bound together by common opinion and desires but are too numerous for each to maintain personal relations with the others.

The public is an aggregation of persons, moving in a common universe of discourse, confronted by an issue or a value divided in their opinion regarding ways to meet the issue or to appraise the value and engaging in discussion.

According to Kimball Young an opinion is a belief somewhat stronger or more intense than a mere notion or impression but less strong than positive knowledge based on complete or adequate proof.Opinions is really a belief about some serious topic. Opinion implies careful thought and consideration. It is founded on some kind of information or evidence. It is not necessary that opinion should always be correct.

According to John Dewey public opinion is judgement which is formed and entertained by those who constitute the public and is about public affairs. Morris Ginberg says by public opinion is meant the mass of ideas and judgements operative in a community which are more or less definitely formulated and have a certain stability and are felt by the people who entertain or hold them to be social in the sense that they are a result of many minds acting in common. James T Young writes public opinion is a social judgment of a self-conscious community on a question of general importance after rational public discussion.

Main Features

Public opinion is concerned with a matter of public importance. It is not concerned with the interests of particular group of people.

Public opinion is for social welfare. The welfare of society is an essential characteristic of public opinion.

Public opinion is arrived at after careful thought. It is the tentative deliberative adjustment of public to a situation. It is the logical view of things. Kimball Young is of the view that an opinion maybe rational or based upon some conviction or it may proceed from feeling and emotion.

It is the product of interaction of human minds.

Public opinion is related to a particular age or times .it is to be evaluated in the context of a particular situation.

Public opinion has a cultural base. The culture of a society influences public opinion.

Numbers are not necessary to constitute public opinion. A majority is not enough an unanimity is not required but the opinion must be such that while the minority may not share it they feel bound by conviction not by fear to accept it.

Public opinion may be defined as the opinion of the people held by them on any issue for the welfare of the whole community .It is a collective product. It is an opinion in which the public finds itself for any reason constrained. Public opinion is always moving toward a decision even though it never is unanimous.

The Formation of Public Opinion

There are three stages in the formation of public opinion- The rise of an issue-discussion and proposed solutions and arrival at a consensus. As soon as a public issue emerges there is usually a preliminary phase of discussion. The issue is defined and a hope is expressed for its solution. Later as a discussion continues those concerned express their own views on the issue and propose various and often divergent solutions through letters, petitions, memoranda etc.In the course of time we pass on the third stage when opinion begins to crystallize and people began to take sides.

The formation of public opinion depends upon a number of factors. Symbols play a most important role in the process of forming opinions. Symbols are combination of words, personalities, music, drama and other such devices that make an impression upon the masses. They may be slogans or they may be factors linked to popular sentiments which arouse the imagination and cause individuals to respond readily as democracy,liberty,red,fair deal, pearl harbour.

All these are omnibus words or symbols carrying vague general meanings but which have specific meanings for particular groups. They are appealing symbols, devices to reduce discussion through associating an idea with a good or bad subject and thus to get the individual to approve or reject a proposal without examining the evidence. These words move the people and lead them to action.

Symbols are more effective with people whose basic predispositions are already in tune with the propaganda themes. Thus people with conservative predispositions would be less liberal than those with liberal predispositions. The formation of opinion tends in large measures to be the result of the previous experiences and attitudes. A large number of people are indifferent to public affairs. They have little leisure time for consideration of public affairs. They usually accept ready-made opinion from others. Though they neither make opinion as thinkers nor help to mould it as critics they swell its volume. Thus the opinion which originates with the few is communicated to the many who transform it into public opinion. The continuous advocacy of the opinion by the minority group leads the majority to believe that the opinion may be fairly universal and adopt it as their own and thus a public opinion is formed.

The Propaganda

The term propaganda is defined as the purveying of lies by conscienceless writers and speakers. It the communication of distorted ideas or inadequate facts or both conveyed in a manner or tone so as to create in the object of propaganda an emotional response favourable to the implicit bias of the propagandist.

According to Clyde R Miller propaganda is the attempt to influence others to some predetermined end by appealing to their thought and feeling.

According to Anderson and Parker propaganda is the deliberate use of communication to induce people to favour one predetermined line of thought or action over another.

Kimball Young writes for our purposes we shall define propaganda as the more or less deliberate planned and systematic use of symbol chiefly through suggestion and related psychological techniques with a view first to altering and controlling opinions, ideas and values and ultimately to changing overt action along predetermined lines.

Propaganda is the use of reasoning or facts in order to persuade another person to favour a particular kind of action that he would otherwise not favour. However propaganda is not necessarily the propagation of wrong views by questionable methods. Groups and organizations whose objectives have been socially constructive have often resorted to the method of propaganda. The Family Planning Dept in order to control the birth rate has used all the devices of propaganda.

Propaganda is a powerful force. In modern times it has come to play an important role. The modern world is dependent on it. The govt, business houses, the political parties and various other sections of society use it so serve their own purposes. In the two world wars the battle on the propaganda front was as intense as on the military front. During the freedom struggle in India the Congress Party carried intensive propaganda to promote anti-British feelings.

Propaganda can be useful to bring about a change in the policy of the government. In India the propaganda against dowry and sex distinctions led the govt of India to enact laws prohibiting dowry and giving equal rights to women in the matter of inheritance. The propaganda against compulsory sterilization forced the govt to change not only its policy regarding family planning programme but also the name of the Ministry from the Ministry of Family Planning to Ministry for Family Welfare.

The Govt also uses propaganda to win people's cooperation for implementing its policies and programmes. Thus the family planning programme was widely publicised and vast propaganda machinery was mobilised to influence the people in its favour. Propaganda is a powerful instrument to bring about social change. It is difficult to change the habits and attitudes of the people. The propagandist through psychological aids goes directly to the springs of motivation. Propaganda is an important medium for transmitting those pressures which help in breaking the bonds of the traditional social order.

Propaganda has played a very useful role during war time. In both the world wars both sides made wide use of propaganda. It helps in crushing the morale of the army and civil population in the enemy state and in building up the morale of the army and civil population in one's own state.

Remarkably, thus the state in modern times cannot do without propaganda.

Propaganda is a means of influencing people. It is as old as the human group and has been employed at all times and on all cultural levels. Psychological warfare is the use of propaganda against an enemy through the employment of modern media of mass communications together with such other operational measures and devices of a military, economic or political nature as may be required to supplement propaganda for the purpose of reaching mass audiences in order to persuade them to accept certain beliefs and ideas.

It is used to undermine the enemy's resistance, to dissuade neutrals from joining the other side or to encourage friends and others. The value of psychological warfare as a technique of propaganda is yet unknown.

Soreno points out that this kind of warfare depends on the skill and ability of the warrior to understand the problems of the enemy or target people and their patterns of thought and action and to affect them with all the means at his disposal.

Appendix

ANALYSIS OF SOCIAL MOVEMENTS

[This analysis of social movement is taken from write-up of illustrious Indian sociologist Dr. T.K. Oommen, which will be haighly informative to all researchers in sociology and social sciences. —Author]

Bhoodan-Gramdan Movement

The Bhoodan-Gramdan movement, began in 1951, a year before the Community Development Programme (CDP) was launched by the Government of India. These were then viewed by many as alternative approaches to socio-economic reconstruction of rural India. By the time I began my research in 1962, several social scientists had written extensively on CDP and most of these studies had been sponsored and financed by the different agencies of the government. But even a decade after its inception, hardly any researcher had made a serious attempt to evaluate the impact of the Bhoodan-Gramdan movement, although it was (and still is) the only agrarian movement in independent India with an all-India spread. However, this movement did generate some interest, as it was an attempt to reconstruct Indian rural society relying on voluntaristic action, and of faith in the goodness of human nature.

It attracted the attention of a few foreign writers, none of whom was a social scientist, who characterised it in an idyllic fashion; the movement to them was a 'miracle' and a 'superhuman' achievement which could happen only in Gandhi's India (see Tennyson 1955; Dev Vasto 1956; Hoffman 1961). Two social scientists, a foreigner (Yinger 1957) and an Indian (Sekher 1968), attempted an evaluation of the movement, based on secondary data, at the macro level. No investigation of the impact of the movement at the grass-roots, its real target, had been undertaken by any researcher, foreign or Indian. Therefore, I thought of studying the 'Sociology of *Gramdan* Villages'.

When I started my research in 1962, the air was thick with the purported 'success' of the movement; the national press and All India Radio regularly reported its progress and the Planning Commission published statistics relating to the collection and distribution of land through the movement, in its evaluation of land reforms in India. Official patronage was readily extended to the movement and was very visible. Even the United Nations' documents on land reforms made references to the success of the movement.

At that time, two sets of questions figured in my mind. The first set included the following: why was it that no sociologist had ventured to make a through analysis of the movement, thereby either vindicating or contradicting the prevalent popular and official opinions and claims about the movement? Such a study had great potentialities for building a theory of rural social transformation not only for India, but perhaps for other developing countries as well. Further, such a study could have helped in examining the efficacy or inadequacy of several social policy measures initiated by the governments in developing countries to bring about rural social change. Why was it that such an opportunity was missed?

I do not intend to catalogue all possible reasons for this serious omission but let me list a few. First was the intellectual claustrophobia created by the professional conservatism of Indian sociologists. During the 1950s and the 1960s Indian sociologists studied religion, caste, family, village and urban communities. Any deviation from these 'sacred themes' was not only discouraged but even ridiculed. Second, as the movement drew its inspiration from the *sarvodaya* (literally, upliftment of all) ideology propounded by Mohandas Karamchand Gandhi and as it was initiated by Acharya Vinoba Bhave, his foremost disciple, most social scientists dismissed the movement as 'conservative' and hence not worth studying. Third, given the state patronage extended to and accepted by the movement, it came to be identified with the government and the party in power. Admittedly, the movement did not operate as a countervailing power to the state and therefore it did not attract much attention. Fourth, the movement was avowedly non-violent and hence non-controversial, had no nuisance value and hence did not attract the attention of the law and order agencies. Finally, hardly any material incentive in the form of financial assistance or a possible career advantage was available to those who could have undertaken the study.

The second set of questions were comparative in nature: If the movement was successful in certain regions or villages in tackling the basic agrarian problem of India, namely redistribution of land in favour of the tiller, what conditions favoured it? Were these conditions replicable elsewhere? And, if these conditions were recreated in areas where the movement was absent or unsuccessful, will it then spread to the entire countryside, thereby solving one of India's crucial problems: the concentration of land in the hands of a small proportion of absentee and non-cultivating landlords? I don't think that it is a *post factum* rationalisation to state that while my enquiry was primarily motivated by intellectual curiosity it also had an indirect practical concern, namely the improvements of the lot of the rural poor, the landless agricultural labourers. This in turn moulded the content of my study.

Since I set out to study the impact of the Bhoodan-Gramdan movement at the grass-roots it was necessary to investigate whether its ideology had been adequately disseminated among *gramdan* villagers, the strength of their motivation to donate villages-in-gift, the economic and political changes in these villages following *gramdan,* the role of local leadership in effecting these changes (if changes did occur), and the value-orientations of the villagers.

As I proceeded with the investigation of *gramdan* villages I discovered that a meaningful analysis of the movement was possible only by conscious effort to view the village situation against the backdrop of the functioning of the movement at the macro level. Understandably, my initial theme, 'Sociology of *gramdan* Villages' changed to 'Ideology and Social Change'. Broadly speaking, the movement had three layers: the micro (village and district), the macro (national) and the meso (state) levels. The macro level supplied the ideology, the broad organisational pattern and the top leadership; the meso level subjected the first two dimensions to a filtration process and moulded them to suit local conditions.

For example, in states with a sizeable tribal population, *gramdan* rather than *bhoodan* was accorded greater importance considering the traditional tribal pattern of communal land-ownership. At the micro level the ideology was translated into actual programmes through organisations inducted into the system for the purpose. This realisation led to a further shift in the emphasis of my study. While retaining the focus of investigation on *gramdan* villages, I started concentrating on the role of ideology in bringing about change which necessitated a macro-level analysis of the movement as well.

As I became familiar with the available writings on the emergence of the movement (Ramabhai 1958, 1962), I found that its origin and spread could not be attributed solely to its ideology. During the pre-independence days Gandhi's *sarvodaya* ideology had been overshadowed by the nationalist preoccupation with the goal of *swaraj* (independence). Its tenets had scarcely been translated into concrete action, particularly in dealing with inequality in land distribution. Further, the movement needed a style of functioning, different from that of the anti-colonial struggle, and yet acceptable and appealing to the people. This was precisely what Vinoba attempted and his style of functioning was that of a charismatic leader. Taking my cue from this, I finally reformulated the theme of my study as 'Charismatic Movements and Social Change'. At that point I had simply assumed, following Max Weber, that charisma was a system-changing force in society. But by the time I concluded my study I had become convinced that charisma could as well be a system stabilising force and hence the title of the book: *Charisma, Stability and Change.* In the book, I first attempted a general analysis of the movement in India based on its origin, ideology, organisation and macro-leadership pattern before presenting details of its functioning at the grass-roots level in the *gramdan* villages of Rajasthan.

Based on this experience, I suggest that analyses of social movements should comprise two aspects, the macro and the micro. By the macro-dimension of movement I mean its ideology contained in the written and unwritten pronouncements by the leaders; organisation, the machinery through which the ideology is sought to be propagated and communicated; strategy and tactics, the specific programmes, organisational devices and procedures adopted to put its ideology into practice. The micro-dimension refers to its actual operation and its consequences at the grass-roots level, wherein we observe the filtration or accretion process to which the ideology and organisation are subjected, in order to meet specific local conditions and the mechanisms through which the movement ideology is put into practice. Thus, an analysis of the macro-dimension of a movement informs us of its ideology and organisation, a study of the micro-dimension acquaints us with its actual functioning on the ground; the former offers us a perspective from above and the latter a view from below. In order to arrive at a meaningful understanding of a movement, then, we should view it from both these angles. And this is precisely what I attempted to do in the case of the Bhoodan-Gramdan movement, although my initial intention was to analyse the movement only from a micro viewpoint.

My analysis of the macro-dimension of the movement added new aspects to the study. In the case of the Bhoodan-Gramdan movement most of its basic tenets were contained in Gandhi's *sarvodaya* philosophy. In analysing the ideology of the movement I drew upon the writings of its chief theoreticians—Gandhi, Vinoba Bhave, and Jayaprakash Narayan. Similarly, I found that its organisational core had pre-dated the emergence of the movement in its present form—the Akhil Bharat Sarva Seva Sangh (All India Social Service Society). When the movement started functioning as a concrete programme for the collection and distribution of land, the need for a specific new organisation was keenly felt. In fact, soon after the first land donation in 1951 in Pochampalli village in Andhra Pradesh, Vinoba constituted a 'trust'—a tripartite committee consisting of the donor, local influentials and *sarvodaya* workers—to administer land distribution. As the number of donations multiplied, the need for coordinating organisational tasks arose. Thus, village, district, state and national level organisations developed gradually. Generally speaking, except at the village level, coordination of the movement activities had been taken over by the existing *sarvodaya* organisations. Therefore, it was necessary to analyse the organisational innovations of the movement at the village level in order to understand the problems of translating the movement ideology into practice.

Another 'feed-back' from the field provided the rationale for the shift in the focus of the study. My analysis of the communication pattern revealed that most of the villagers viewed Vinoba Bhave, the initiator of the movement, as a saint-on-march; they were gifting away their lands to a saint! Further, while analysing the local leadership pattern of the movement, I observed a process of vertical transmission of charisma; local charismatic heroes donned the mantle of charisma and adopted a style of life akin to that of the national leaders and maintained their appeal through contact-charisma. This led me to conclude that the change propelling force in the movement was not so much its ideology as it was the charismatic appeal of the national and local leaders. I became convinced of the tremendous importance of the charismatic resource to mobilise people into collective actions. It was this realisation which emboldened me to stick to the new focus of the study, 'Charismatic Movements and Social Change'. The point I want to emphasise is this: even as a researcher starts with a specific plan of study, the focus of his investigation is likely to change as he interacts with the field. What important is his flexibility and ability to respond to the demands of the field situation.

An indirect pay-off due to successive shifts in the focus of study needs to be noted here. As indicated above, the analysis of the movement at the macro level showed the existence of an ideology and an organisational core prior to the emergence an spread of the movement in its present form. The critical factor facilitating the movement's spread was charismatic leadership. This led me to conclude that we could identify distinct aspects of any movement for purposes of analysis: ideology, organisation and leadership. Any of these dimensions may emerge first and other aspects would crystallise subsequently. This led to the formulation of the life-cycle approach to the study of movements. Inevitably, a given aspect of a movement may have primacy over the other aspects at a specific point of time. If this is so, we can speak of three types of movements depending on which of these aspects emerges first in its life-cycle: ideological, organisational or charismatic, a typology I proposed in the study.

Reflecting back on the life-cycle approach proposed and the typology formulated based on that, I note two major omissions. First, I failed to account for the societal conditions which facilitated or thwarted the emergence of a particular type of movement. This lacuna emanated from the failure to systematically link the theory of social movements with a theory of social structure. A more fruitful analysis could be attempted by focusing on the system conditions more systematically. The crucial question then to be posed in a study of movements is: What type of movement emerges in what kind of society and why?

Second, I had overlooked the importance of analysing the mobilisational activities of the movement. The main reason for this was the style of the movement itself. In the case of the Bhoodan-Gramdan movement, the most important mobilisational activity was *padayatra* (walking a long distance) by movement workers to propagate its ideology and to collect donations of land. Apart from this, the movement, attempted very little mobilisational activity, partly because of the absence of any organised opposition to it. The cause the movement championed, land to the tiller, had been accepted by the government and most of the political parties. Further, the movement mobilised support by adopting non-violent means. Hence, there were no major confrontations between the supporters of the movement and their opponents and therefore mobilisation was not a particularly exciting area of analysis. However, analysis of mobilisation in a social movement is too important an area to be neglected.

As a young student initiated into the world of social research, my immediate problem was the focus of study. Although my field investigation was to be done in *gramdan* (village-in-gift) villages, my aim was not to analyse the social structure of these villages, or even to understand the style of life of the villagers. My purpose was to evaluate the role of the Bhoodan movement to bring about social change and to observe the manifestations of this in *gramdan* villages. Therefore, the questions that arose in my mind were: How can one establish whether the changes, if any, taking place in *gramdan* villages are exclusively, or at least predominantly, due to the movement? Second, assuming that there are multiple causes of change, how can we isolate the specific contribution made by the movement in effecting changes in *gramdan* villages?

The fact that I began my investigation with a definite purpose called for the employment of an 'experimental' research design. It is widely recognised that a study of change is methodologically sound only if it is attempted either in a time perspective or in a space perspective. While in the former case the same working universe is subjected to analysis through time, the latter calls for a comparative study of at least two spatial units with the provision that the additional variable assumed to be causing the change is absent from one of the units. Since the Bhoodan-Gramdan movement was in existence barely for a decade when I started studying it in 1962 and, further, that the villages actually selected for the study were *gramdan* villages only for five or less number of years, it was felt to be unrewarding to attempt an analysis of *gramdan* villages, in a time perspective. Therefore, I decided to study two sets of villages, *gramdan* (experimental) and non-*gramdan* (Control), in order to understand the changes in the former set of villages, which may be attributed to the movement.

Since the movement operated all over India and over 5,000 villages were donated in *gramdan* by 1961, it was necessary to decide upon a specific locale from which the villages were to be selected. I cannot offer any specific rationale for selecting Rajasthan as the locale of my study, except that it was convenient as I was attached to one of the universities in that state at the time. However, discussion with movement leaders revealed that Rajasthan was one of the states wherein the movement was active and 'successful'. In 1961 there were 234 *gramdan* villages in Rajasthan and I had to select a few villages for intensive observation. Although a complete list of these villages was obtained from the coordinating agency of the movement in the state, the Rajasthan Sarva Seva Sangh, most of them could not be located or if located the requisite data to facilitate the selection of villages was not available. Therefore, I decided to select a few villages from among the 63 *gramdan* villages brought under the purview of legislation, the Rajasthan

Gramdan Act, 1960, since some preliminary information was available about these villages. Thus, the further delimitation of villages for selection to be included in the study was based on another social factor, namely, availability of data. The third social factor which influenced the selection of villages was limited resources—time and money. I was expected to finish this specific research assignment within a period of three years and funds available at my disposal were extremely limited, both of which restricted the scope of my study in terms of coverage.

These social factors apart, a few research issues conditioned the selection of specific villages. An examination of the details relating to the 65 *gramdan* villages brought under the Act revealed that these villages were, generally speaking, atypical, viewed in terms of their size of population and/or number of households, the area of land held by the villagers and social complexity viewed in terms of the number of the social categories, castes and tribes, found in these villages, as compared with non-*gramdan* villages. There was yet another factor which contributed to the atypicality of *gramdan* villages. In the process of becoming *gramdan* villages they have undergone a process of bifurcation, usually in terms of the village 'core' and the hamlets. Thus, if a 'revenue' village had three hamlets, apart from the village core, as a result of *gramdan* four 'villages' emerged out of it. The search for *gramdan* villages similar in size and social structural complexity as compared with non-*gramdan* villages, prompted me to select as far as possible unbifurcated villages. If I were to select typical *gramdan* villages they would have been atypical villages of Rajasthan. Thus, the *gramdan* villages selected were more or less typical of the villages of the region but were atypical *gramdan* villages.

The villages selected were atypical from another angle too. I wanted to examine the conditions which led to the successful operation of *gramdan* villages as communitarian enterprises, because the assumption was that the replication of these conditions in other villages would facilitate their being brought under *gramdan*. Therefore it was necessary to select 'successful cases' and this was precisely what I did. In consultation with the movement leaders at the local level I made a list of successful *gramdan* villages from the pool of 'typical' villages for closer analysis. Thus, the theoretical purpose and practical concerns of my study dictated the selection of *gramdan* villages.

A final consideration which conditioned the selection of *gramdan* villages was their spatial spread. On examination of the relevant data I found that out of the 65 *gramdan* villages brought under the purview of legislation, 62 were located in five of the 26 districts of Rajasthan and I decided to confine the selection of villages to these five *gramdan* 'clusters'. In turn, these five districts belonged to three major regions of the state—the Eastern Plain, the Dry (Arid) Zone and the Southern Highland. Two of the *gramdan* clusters each belonged to the Dry and Highland Areas and one to the Plain Area.

I decided to select one village each from three regions. In the case of the Plain area, since there was only one *gramdan* cluster, I faced no problem of selection. But there were two clusters each in the case of Dry and Highland regions and I settled on one or another of the clusters depending on certain practical considerations: relatively easy accessibility to the village, amenability of the movement leaders at the district level, etc.

However, the problem I had to tackle in the selection

of villages was not yet over, as 12 per cent of *gramdan* villages brought under the Act were new colonies, villages established on land donated by local landlords or on government land. Since these colonies were established *de novo*, I anticipated their functioning to be on a different footing, as traditional animosities based on neighbourhood and factions may not be present in these villages. In order to give representation to this category I selected a fourth villages (a new colony) from the Highland region in which the incidence of new colonies was the highest. Thus, I selected four 'successful' *gramdan* villages, which were also unbifurcated typical revenue villages, from four out of the five districts to which most of these villages belonged, the districts being drawn from the three major regions of the state. It may be noted here that the selection of villages from the three regions also facilitated the inclusion of villages with different sizes, quality of land and varying social composition (castes and tribes) in the study.

While four *gramdan* villages were selected only three *non-gramdan* villages need be selected because the category of new colonies was non-existent in the case of non-*gramdan* (control) villages. The three control villages were selected from the same districts, *talukas* and *panchayats* as that of the experimental cases, the distance between them ranging from five to ten miles in all cases. The selection of both the experimental and control cases from the same administrative units was intended to neutralise the impact of state-initiated programmes like Community Development and Panchayati Raj. The use of an experimental design thus affected the choice of control villages because of the need to select two sets of villages, the control set being comparable to the experimental set except in regard to the additional factor, namely, *gramdan*. Although sufficient care was taken to ensure similarity between experimental and control cases in regard to landholding pattern, size of population and social structural features, there were some differences between them. This is an inherent limitation in applying the experimental design to a natural setting. Thus, the control villages had more households, their complexity greater in terms of the number of social categories and the inequality of landholdings more telling as compared with their *gramdan* counterparts. However, these differences, I am sure, were not so crucial as to abandon the design itself. At any rate, instead of adopting a 'methodologically naked' design. I thought it was necessary to attempt a rigorous comparison since my purpose was to understand the rate and directionality of change.

I did not begin my fieldwork with an 'open mind'. The very fact that I had decided on the broad area of my investigation before-hand, made it incumbent on me to have an outline of what I was looking for in the field. The impression conveyed by some researchers which can be stated as: 'I went (to the field), I observed and I analysed', is to my mind quite contrary to the 'natural' research process. On the other hand, the way in which one presents one's argument and data may impart the impression that the author started with a preconceived framework. For instance, readers of *Charisma, Stability and Change* may get the impression that I started with the argument stated in Chapter 1 and collected 'convenient data' to 'prove' my argument. This is quite contrary to my experience in evolving my strategy. I stated my argument at the very outset, in order to inform the presentation of data with some consistency and order. In fact, the argument, although stated in the beginning of the book, was the end product of my research.

I started with the assumption, as noted earlier, that

charisma is a change generating force in societies. Similarly, it was my hunch in the beginning that charismatic endowment existed only at the macro level, that it was a quality to be found only among the national-level leaders of the movement. Although I started with these assumptions and hypotheses it was possible to float counter-hypotheses, not always in a cut and dried fashion but as a sort of 'mental experiment'. Thus, in effect there was a constant interaction between the assumption that I entertained, the concepts I employed and the empirical evidence I gathered. It was through this process that I arrived at my argument whose guiding principle was neither deduction nor induction but retroduction. Let me elaborate.

I gained my initial insight in characterising the movement as 'charismatic' from the descriptions of the conditions under which the first land-gift was obtained and Vinoba's *response* to it (Rambhai 1958, 1962). However, as soon as I undertook my first field trip the empirical manifestation of charisma became clearer to me. The incidence of *gramdan* villages was high along the route of Vinoba's *padayatra;* the people were gifting away their land to a peripatetic saint. But gradually I noticed that the charismatic quality was also attributed to, or found in the regional—and village-level leaders as well and hence I started working with the notion of local or 'little charismatics'. The local leaders of the movement were often looked upon as charismatic heroes by the people, linking them with national ones. For instance, I came across Bagad Gandhi (Bagad being a folk region constituted by Dungarpur and Banswara districts of Rajasthan) and little Vinobas and Gandhis even at the village level. In the light of this evidence I postulated that there were two types of local charismatic leaders: (a) Those who came to don the mantle of charisma independently of the leaders of the wider system. This possibility obtained in systems in which leaders operated independently of the wider context, their independence being rooted in the cultural autonomy of their systems: (b) The mantle of charisma may be passed downward by the macro-level leader by grooming regional or local leaders or the latter may establish sufficient communication with the former thereby assuming the role of his spokesman at the local level. This vertical dispersion of charisma was designated contact-charisma.

The notion of local charismatics also led to a reformulation of the attributes of charisma. While the local leaders emulated the life-style of macro leaders in their dress, dietary practices and daily work schedule, they operated in a very limited locale. They were in constant interaction with the people and it was not possible to create a smoke-screen and mystify the relations between the leaders and the followers. Admittedly, we would search in vain for the charismatic qualities of a Gandhi or Vinoba in a local charismatic leader. Therefore, I argued that charisma was an amorphous attribute qualitatively different at different levels and contexts. I then reformulated the notion of charisma as follows: 'The attributes of charisma are not given for ever, they are contextual. That is to say, charisma is ultimately a product of social structure and it undergoes qualitative transformation concomitant to the changes in the nature of society' (Oommen 1972a: 6).

Another insight I gained from the application of the concept of charisma to a specific empirical context was the system-stabilising function of charisma. Analysis of charismatic authority was crucial to Weber's explanations of social change. Within the framework of German historicism, Weber sought to explain the problem of change at the macro level through the concept of charisma. The charismatic leaders were innovators and creators who cause large-scale change, whom Weber distinguished from the maintainers of tradition. But I found that the means a leader employs would render him a charismatic hero even if he proved to be an agent of system stability. Further, I observed that the leaders of the Bhoodan-Gramdan movement were instrumental for system-conservation, at least in certain respects (Oommen 1967: 88-89). Vinoba wanted to establish a society from which exploitation was rooted out, through peaceful means. Party because of his approach to change, the movement could not effectively confront vested interests and unwittingly even reinforced them. Thus, in spite of its charismatic force, the movement often led to the perpetuation of the system.

Another instance of the bearing of empirical research on concept formation may be noted here. The prevalent tendency in community power structure analysis was to emphasise a given approach—positional, reputational or decisional—in locating influentials which often led to the failure to net all the leaders in an analytical framework (Oommen 1970b: 226-39). I employed all the approaches to locate the leaders in the villages studied. In *gramdan* villages there were two important formal bodies, the executive committee of the *gram sabha* (village assembly), making routine decisions and the Assembly itself constituted by all adults in the village, those who were above 18 years, in which the ultimate authority for local affairs was vested. The usual practice in the executive committee was to get the decisions endorsed by *all* its members who appended their signatures or thumb impressions. But the *gram sabha* meetings were too unwieldy to collect signatures of all present and, therefore, they were collected only from a limited number of persons. The significant point to observe was, *who* were the persons from whom signatures were collected and what were *the bases* on which they were qualified to sign. In one of the *gram sabha* meetings at which I was present, the secretary of the executive committee was collecting signatures from a few additional individuals *other than* the executive committee members. On enquiry I was told that these were *khas admis* (men who matter) in the context of village affairs. Such observations led me to a fuller understanding of the nature of the power structure in villages on the basis of which I made the following formulations:

1. All those who wield real power, *power reservoirs,* in a village community may not be on the formal decision-making bodies.
2. The *power exercisers* who constitute the formal decision-making structures have legal or formal power but they may not wield actual power.
3. The *power pool* in a community is constituted by power reservoirs and exercisers.
4. A power exerciser may be able to use his position to become a power reservoir but one can be a member of the power reservoir without being a power exerciser. That is, membership in formal bodies is a resource for acquiring actual power, but actual power can be acquired independent of formal structure.
5. If the power reservoirs are not power exercisers or if the power exercisers are not falling in line with the power reservoirs, political instability is likely.
6. Political stability is assured when power reservoirs are also power exercisers or power exercisers are controlled by power reservoirs.

Thus, an empirical observation in the field yielded fresh insights about the nature of the power structure and political instability.

The point here is that even as a researcher starts with a conceptual framework, it undergoes constant revision as he confronts empirical reality. The field situation offers him opportunities to reformulate existing concepts and invest them with new meanings, if he has the required flexibility and openness. Additionally, the field situation also continuously provides the researcher the context for enunciating new concepts.

Agrarian Movement in Kerala

The three very well-known approaches in history to tackle agrarian problems are: violent uprising by deprived peasantry, legislative intervention by the state and voluntaristic non-violent action. A large number of studies on the impact of land reforms initiated by the government were completed in India by the 1960s, particularly by economists. Having analysed the Bhoodan-Gramdan movement in India, the best-known non-violent effort in history to tackle agrarian problems, I came to the conclusion that in terms of its announced aim of establishing communitarian villages based on collective land-ownership, the movement was an abortive experiment. Even since, I had been wanting to study an agrarian movement with a different orientation in rural India. An opportunity emerged in the late 1960s.

With the ushering in of the so-called 'Green Revolution' in India, the role of economic development in accentuating income disparities became a favourite theme of social science research. The widespread agrarian unrest in India's countryside, culminating in the emergence of the violent

Naxalbari revolt in West Bengal in 1967, released shock waves throughout India. Unlike the non-violent Sarvodaya movement, the Naxalbari uprising was widely discussed, debated and analysed. Everybody seemed to be attesting to the presumed linkage between the Green Revolution and rural unrest. Even the then Home Minister articulated the popular stereotype when he declared in Parliament that the Green Revolution will turn into a red one if the strategy of rural change was not immediately reoriented.

Having followed this debate carefully for some time I made an initial effort to contest the widely heralded hypothesis, based on the data available in the Home Ministry report (Oommen 1971c: 99-103). I suggested that the presumed causal linkage between the Green Revolution and agrarian unrest was naive, simplistic and was not sustainable. But it was necessary to explicate my position with hard and detailed empirical data. My native district, Alleppey, in Kerala, provided an excellent empirical context to pursue the analysis. Although an Intensive Agricultural Development Project (IADP) district, Alleppey scarcely experienced the Green Revolution. On the other hand, Alleppey had a long tradition of agrarian unrest, very high agricultural wage-rate and low productivity. My detailed and intensive study of the district conclusively proved that the presumed causal sequential explanation; Development → Disparity → Discontent → Conflict, was facile and misleading. I found that mobilisation of the peasantry and agrarian proletariat by a multiplicity of political parties competing for clients, substantially contributed to agrarian conflicts (Oommen 1971a: 229-68).

Given my interest in rural social transformation and familiarity with rural India favourably responded to a request from the Food and Agricultural Organisation (FAO) of the United Nations in 1972 to undertake a study of agrarian organisations in one of the districts, as a part of a wider study covering 20 districts from all over India. Without hesitation I selected Alleppey district. The purpose of the FAO study was to collect and analyse data on agrarian organisations keeping in mind what factors facilitate or obstruct the building of organisations for the welfare of the rural poor.

I came across a large number and a wide variety of agrarian organisations in Alleppey. From the perspective of building organisations for the welfare of the rural poor, they could be classified into two: those sponsored by the government and those initiated by political parties. The archetype of the first being Harijan co-operatives and of the second being peasant and agricultural labour unions. In terms of their aims, while the cooperatives were dismal failures, the unions were a thumping success. One of the main reasons which accounted for this differential performance was the nature of leadership in these organisations. I therefore argued that it cooperatives were entrusted to the leaders who organised labour unions they may perform better (Oommen 1976: 177-96).

The FAO study clearly revealed the importance of agrarian unions in bringing about substantial change in rural Kerala. For a fuller understanding it was necessary to analyse their style of operation. This called for a new study. If the FAO study concentrated on the organisational dimension, the focus of the new investigation had to be mobilisation.

As I have noted earlier in the Bhoodan movement study, the mobilisational dimension was neglected, partly because it was a non-violent movement. But in Kerala, what characterised the functioning of agricultural labour unions was their frequent confrontations with farmers' associations. Understandably, the focus in this study was on the varieties of mobilisations by a multiplicity of agrarian unions and associations.

Given the findings of my initial study of Alleppey district which dispelled the causal linkage between the Green Revolution and agrarian unrest, I was persuaded to enlarge the scope of my new study. The following questions became pertinent. Was there a tradition of peasant movement in Kerala? If yes, when did it emerge and crystallise? Were there basic differences in this tradition among the three regions—Tranvancore, Cochin and Malabar—which came to constitute Kerala? If so, what were the bases of the differences? What was the relationship between peasant mobilisation and anti-colonial struggle? What changes, if any, did the agrarian movement undergo after independence? Which parties and organisations took the lead in mobilising different agrarian classes? How did the collective actors define and perceive their identities and what were the consequences of this cognition? What was the impact of state policies in determining the course of agrarian movement?

Having stumbled on the idea of career of a movement (the life-cycle approach) while studying the Bhoodan movement, I was inclined to pursue the same strand of analysis in the case of the Kerala agrarian movement too. While the Bhoodan movement had a rather short career, that of the agrarian movement in Kerala was long and eventful. Further, while the former was initiated by a charismatic personality at the national level and had subsequently spread to distant parts of the country, the Kerala agrarian movement was autonomous to begin with but was subsequently linked to all-India movements (e.g., the colonial movement) and structures (e.g., political parties).

Given the fact that I was studying a movement which survived and continued for nearly a century, a question arose as to whether the nature of the movement remained the same throughout its existence. This prompted me to examine closely the goal transformations, value orientations, the nature of enemies and the styles of mobilisation in the different phases of the movement. Based on this analysis, the movement was divided into four major historical phases: the pre-political, the anti-colonial, the anti-Congress and the pro-government phases. It is necessary to briefly explain the rationale behind this classification.

The pre-political peasant revolts and rebellions usually had independent local origins and were rarely coordinated at the regional level. Notwithstanding their economic goals these revolts were characterised by primordial collectivisms. Their ideology, organisation weapon and leadership were closely linked to and utilised the symbols of caste and religious collectivities. They were rarely exclusively agrarian in content and most of these movements were also cultural revolts. That is, an undifferentiated social structure gives birth to an amorphous 'agrarian' movement with multiple goals.

The anti-colonial phase was distinct in several specific ways:

1. Coordination of the movement on a wider, almost on an all-India basis.
2. Confrontation with a clearly identified and hierarchically ordered set of enemies, namely, the British, the 'feudal'/absentee landlord, the money-lender and the big landlord.

3. Emergence of political parties with distinct pro-landlord anti-peasant, and anti-landlord pro-peasant orientations.

In the first decade of independent India the peasant movement of Kerala was explicitly anti-government for the following reasons: First, the mobilisation of peasantry and agrarian proletariat was undertaken mainly by the Communist Party of India, which was in the opposition. Second, the Congress Party, having acquired power, took or appeared to be taking a pro-landlord posture.

In the fourth phase, beginning with 1957, the Kerala agrarian movement took a different turn as the party or parties which were the chief mobilisers of the peasantry and agrarian proletariat either formed the government (intermittently) or remained as substantial opposition parties with sufficient political clout to challenge the parties in power. This rendered the possibility of the agrarian movement operating as an agent of the establishment and/or extension of the party in power.

The conceptual distinction between party, voluntary association and movement is well-documented and widely accepted in sociology. This conceptualisation is based on the empirical experiences of Western liberal democracies. But these distinctions are scarcely applicable to one-party systems and the Indian political situation. For example, what is labelled as a peasant or agrarian 'movement' in India is invariably the mobilisational activities of agrarian unions, that is, voluntary associations, which are front-organisations of political parties. Viewed thus, if one makes a comprehensive study of the activities of political parties that would encapsulate movement activities too.

In Kerala there are several agrarian front-organisations

based on parties and classes. Thus, a particular political party may sponsor two or more such organisations (and in fact some of them do)—a peasant association and an agricultural labour union—while others may sponsor only one such association or union. The usual tendency among movement analysts is to concentrate on the activities of one set of these associations or unions—farmers' associations, peasant unions, agricultural labour unions—ignoring others, thereby mistaking the part for the whole. In reality, the agrarian movement is constituted by the cooperative and conflicting interactions between and among these unions and associations.

Discussions on the role of the peasantry in the freedom movement in India are viewed from two perspectives: macro-holism and micro-individualism (Oommen 1985: 2-3). The first overemphasises the political content and motivation and the second highlights only the economic grievances and interests of the peasantry. While emphasising the specific attributes and motives of the peasantry, both these perspectives ignore the properties of the situation in which mobilisations take place. In reality, peasant collective action particularly under colonial conditions is largely prompted by political considerations, the aspirations they share with others to move from subjecthood to citizenship. But the concretisation of this aspiration as far as the peasantry is concerned, is to be found in the redressal of its economic hardships. Even as the holistic perspective informs peasant collective action, the individualistic (class-categorical) interests and needs cannot be overlooked. That is, neither macro-holism nor micro-individualism can fully explain peasant involvement in anti-colonial struggles.

The tendency to juxtapose collective protest actions with state actions and hence movements and legislations is widespread in contemporary social science writings of the Western liberal democracies. But this conceptualisation does not adequately portray the empirical realities of either the socialist countries or of the developing countries. The state in these countries not only initiates a series of legislative measures to bring about radical transformation but even sponsors collective actions either to legitimise its measures and/or to accelerate the process of social transformation. Further, legislation itself can be an initiator or indicator of change depending upon the role the state assumes. Keeping these considerations in mind, I tried to highlight the *complementarity* between legislation and movements. That is, legislation plays a pivotal role in order to institutionalise the changes initiated by social movements. Conversely, even when change is initiated through the instrument of law, collective actions become important to legitimise and complete the process of change. One cannot understand and appreciate these observations unless one conceptualises the state's actions and collective actions as complementary, a pay-off obtained by recognising the difference between our empirical situations and that of Western capitalist democracies.

It is widely recognised that the mould for the emergence of movement is provided by relative deprivation, its perception and articulation by the concerned collectivity. In contrast, very little theoretical work exists with regard to the termination of movements. However, it has been proposed that the specific processes which lead to the termination of a movement are: repression, discreditation, co-optation and institutionalisation (Rush and Denisoff 1971: 367).

My analysis clearly showed that no effort was spared in the pre-independent phase and even in the first decade of free India by the then establishments to repress the agrarian movement in Kerala. In spite of this virulent repression the movement gained in strength, notwithstanding temporary setbacks. Therefore, the critical variable is not repression *per se,* but the collective conscience which bestows *legitimacy* on the agent of repression and attributes *illegitimacy* to movement participants. That is, insofar as the state is perceived by the collectivity as a 'legitimate authority' which should repress the 'illegitimate movement' which offends the collective conscience, repression will be an effective instrument for terminating a movement.

On the other hand, if the state is perceived as an illegitimate intruder and/or supporting the vested interests in society, and movement participants are viewed as martyrs to a cause in the wider interests of the collectivity, then repression will not weaken but strengthen the movement. Thus, my analysis unfolds that, ignoring the properties of the situation leads to the formulation of erroneous theoretical propositions.

With the arrival of freedom and transfer of political power from the British to a national government, a critical proportion of people invested the Congress Government with legitimacy. That is why the repression of agrarian movements by the Congress Government was not viewed with the same disdain by the people at large. Conversely, the party in power tried its best to discredit the Communist Party of India (CPI) as it continued to pursue the path of violence. Recognising the changed situation, the CPI opted for a policy of peaceful transition of socialism and entered into an alliance with the progressive bourgeoisie, that is, the party in power. This in turn led to partial co-optation of several movement leaders directly or indirectly into the establishment. But consequent upon the split of the CPI into CPI(R) and CPI(M) and thanks to the latter's refusal to 'cooperate' with the Congress, the possibility of co-opting movement leaders diminished.

As CPI(M) front-organisations continued to be the most persisting factor in keeping the vitality of the agrarian movement high in Kerala, the strategy of co-optation did not produce the desired effect, namely the demise of the movement. That is, in order that discreditation and co-optation be effective means of terminating movements, a series of prerequisites should exist.

As noted earlier, I began the study of agrarian movement in Kerala within the framework of the natural history or life-cycle approach according to which institutionalisation is an inevitable tendency leading to the termination of a movement. Baldly put, the argument runs as follows: the development of an organisation, however rudimentary, is inevitable of the realisation of movement goals. But the emergence of such organisation inevitably sets in motion forces which defeat the very purpose which necessitated it. The instrument—the movement organisation—becomes instrumental in frustrating the very purpose for which it emerged.

Contrary to this conventional theorisation I found enough support in the empirical evidence available to me that there is no inherent tendency towards institutionalisation. Further, even when it occurs, institutionalisation does not necessarily stop or always decelerate the process of mobilisation which is so fundamental and primary to the continuance of a movement. In fact, mobilisation and institutionalisation coexist and the latter may provide new possibilities for mobilisation.

In the late 1960s when I began my study of agrarian unrest in Kerala, the most widely-studied territorial/spatial unit in Indian sociology and social anthropology was the village. But my effort to understand the Bhoodan movement through an investigation of *gramdan* villages revealed that if I were to link the micro-dimensions with those of the macro—ideology, organisational pattern, leadership—I need to go 'beyond the village' as my unit of study. This experience prompted me to consider the viability of a unit of analysis bigger than the village but manageable for doing fieldwork.

In arriving at the appropriate unit of analysis for a study several considerations are relevant. The most important of these are: the theme of the study, the spatial coverage of the phenomenon and its historicity. Generally speaking, a phenomenon such as social movement is rarely confined to a territorial entity such as a village and it may have existed for a long span of time. The Kerala agrarian movement, notwithstanding its independent and autonomous origins in the three regions which came to constitute Kerala—Malabar, Cochin, and Travancore—got coordinated during the freedom struggle and subsequently came to constitute and operate as a single stream with the emergence of Kerala state. Further, insofar as agrarian mobilisation in India are essentially activities of front-organisations of political parties, the macro-dimensions of agrarian movements are linked to a spatial unit bigger than the particular state in which they function. Thus, the agrarian mobilisations in Kerala initiated by parties such as the Communist Party of India (Marxist) (CPIM), Communist Party of India (CPI), and Congress (I), are tempered by the ideology and styles of functioning of these 'all-India' parties.

Once Kerala emerged as a separate state it was possible to attempt the analysis on an all-Kerala basis. But whether or not this could actually be done would depend upon the nature of data available and to be generated. Insofar as one is drawing from various types of records and documents it is possible to construct a picture of mobilisational activities of a given region or state, say of Malabar or Kerala. But in those contexts and/or periods for which the documents are not available and the researcher generates data through field studies, he must confine himself to a very limited spatial unit. Thus, historical analysis usually undertaken on the basis of documents relates to a wider spatial unit as compared with field investigations done by the researcher. And this shift in the unit of analysis was inevitable. While analysing the current phase of the movement about which I had to collect field data, my unit of analysis was one district, namely Alleppey.

It was possible for me to capture a bottom-up view of the contemporary phase of the movement through the field data I have collected. To match this data I had to tap appropriate sources relating to the historical phase of the movement. The most authentic and useful data I could find was the writing by and on grass-root movement activists—biographies, memoirs, 'historical accounts', literary writings (novels, short stories, and dramas)—and informant interviewing, that is, 'oral history'.

An important source of information widely tapped by most researchers is reports by journalists. I have also used this source. But usually journalists report only when (a) the incidents are violent, and (b) political heavy-weights are present on specific occasions. Thus, the routine activities, particularly at the grass-roots, go unreported. An invaluable source to get at these activities are police records, which are usually not accessible to researchers. Fortunately I was permitted to go through the police records and this helped me get a picture of the activities of different agrarian associations on a continuous basis. Once I knew that a particular incident did take place it was possible for me to pursue its investigation by collecting data through other sources. However, there is one disadvantage if one relies exclusively on police accounts of such incidents and activities. The usual tendency (and this seems to be based on official brief) is to concentrate on the activities of those associations and leaders affiliated to the opposition political parties. But given the political situation prevalent in Kerala the associations affiliated to all parties get their 'attention' in turn as they circulate in and out of power. At any rate, the mobilisational activities are usually kept high by a party when it is in the opposition and therefore it is also natural for the police to concentrate on them.

I have defined the event-structure of the movement as the interactions between the different unions and associations. The record of activities kept by them was another important source of data for me. As is well known, the local (village) units of these organisations rarely keep comprehensive accounts of their activities. Even the decisions are taken in informal meetings. Therefore, the data about local units was invariably collected through informant interviewing, the informants being constituted by a pool of persons drawn from all the organisations.

Yet another source of data was the records of government departments of revenue, development, labour and newly-created organisations such as the Industrial Relations Committee (a tripartite committee to process disputes which arose among the between farmers and workers) or Land Tribunals (to settle the disputes between landowners and their tenants).

The foregoing account clearly unfolds that the major chunk of data for the study was drawn from records of various types and informant interviewing (with the help of interview guides devised for different categories of informants). In addition to this, I have had the opportunity to observe specific incidents of mobilisations and meetings of agrarian organisations for nearly a decade, although intermittantly, beginning in the early 1970s, during my several visits to Kerala, ranging from two to eight weeks.

Summing Up

My experiences in undertaking studies of two social movements reveals that a multiplicity of considerations go into the selection of research themes. The researcher may not be conscious of all these factors, particularly in the beginning. But it is rewarding to bring the unconscious elements into the realm of consciousness because that would at least partly reveal the value biases and preferences the researcher has. To be aware and conscious of one's value preferences is the first step in the journey towards objectivity.

There is an inevitable risk in choosing research themes which foment contemporary political and academic controversies. The possibility of getting grafted into one or another camp is fairly high. To take a position independent of the prevalent popular sentiments and opinions calls for tremendous courage and fortitude. And yet, one has to do precisely that if one is to deserve the label of an impartial analyst.

Those who have a definite issue to investigate and questions to answer would invariably begin their empirical studies armed with a conceptual-theoretical framework. But this need not be an intellectual liability if one is sufficiently open, flexible and creative to reformulate one's framework in the light of one's exposure to empirical evidence. That is, while it is not possible to begin research with an 'open mind', one should constantly keep open one's partially-filled mind to provide scope for creative confrontations between concepts, theories and data. The captive mind is not simply a product of Western academic colonialism, but also of the inability to transcend trained incapacity and inappropriate indigenous work habits

[*Acknowledgement:* This chapter is based on experiences of noted sociologist T.K. Oommen. We owe gratitude to the author and publishers both.]

Glossary

Collective Behavior Theory

The dominant school of sociological thought on social movements in the 1940s and 1950s, collective behavior scholars linked movements to such things as riots, crowds, and mass hysteria. Shaped in part by the recent memory of the fascist movements in Germany, Italy and Japan, and by the conformist mood of the 1950s, this school stressed the irrational dimensions of movements and often saw them as potentially dangerous, temporary aberrations in the otherwise smooth-flowing social system. While parallels between movements and other forms of collective behavior are still studied, this dark, irrationalist view of movements has largely been superseded by more complex and varied approaches.

Collective Identity

Collective identity is the name given to the tendency of many social movements to form a group self-image shaped by, but in turn shaping the consciousness of, individual participants. Social movement theorist Alberto Melluci emphasizes that such collective identities are not so much fixed as in process and offers this more specialized definition: "Collective identity is an interactive, shared definition produced by several individuals (or groups at a more complex level)... that must be conceived as a process because it is constructed and negotiated by repeated activation of the relationships that link individuals (or groups) [to the movement]." See Melluci, "The Process of Collective Identity," in Johnston and Klandermans, eds., *Social Movements and Culture* (1995).

Cycles of Protest

A phrase used to note the patterns of rising and falling action experienced by individual movements as well as the tendency of movements to generate other movements in waves of activity and inactivity (or latency). The concept is most closely identified with political scientist Sydney Tarrow, *Struggle, Politics, and Reform: Collective Action, Social Movements, and Cycles of Protest* (1989).

Direct Theory

A term coined by feminist social movement theorist Noël Sturgeon to describe the highly self-conscious process of collective thinking and acting she observed in the anti-nuclear and anti-militarist direct action movement of the late 1970s and early 1980s. Sturgeon argues that the decision-making process and the ritual actions of certain movement groups reflect, shape and enact a democratic political philosophy, a theory of social change and a sense of historical connection to earlier movements. See Sturgeon, "Theorizing Movements: Direct Action and Direct Theory," in Darnvosky, et al. eds., *Cultural Politics and Social Movements* (1995).

Dramaturgical Analysis

A kind of cultural analysis (derived from anthropology, performance studies, or literary studies) applied to the more dramatic, or ritualistic dimensions of movements, working from the analogy that much political activity generally, and social movement action in particular, has highly theatrical elements (i.e., sit-ins, protest marches, civil disobedience involving symbolic breaking of laws or trespassing).

Frames, Framing, Frame Analysis

Deriving originally from the work of sociologist Erving Goffman, *Frame Analysis* (1974), the concept of frames or framing is used in the contexts of some social movement analysis to mean patterns of perception and/or schemata of interpretation employed by social movement participants or social movement organizations viewed collectively. A frame might be imagined as a kind of template or filter that organizes how one processes new information encountered in the world. Frames organize that information based on previously held beliefs or previously shaped patterns of perception and interpretation. See also, H. Johnston, "A Methodology for Frame Analysis," in Johnston and Klandermans, eds. *Social Movements and Culture* (1995).

Grievance

A grievance is the issue (or issues) around which a social movement develops. Grievances stem from a shared perception that a group of individuals is being denied rights, opportunities, proper respect, safety, or some other form of social good simply because of who they are. Newly articulated grievances are generally the focal points around which movements are organized, but initial grievances are frequently elaborated upon and new grievances often emerge as movements evolve.

Marxist Theory

Marxism as an ideology and theory of social change has had an immense impact on the practice and the analysis of social movements. Marxism arose from an analysis of movements structured by conflicts between industrial workers and their capitalist employers in the 19th century. In the twentieth century a variety of neo-Marxist theories have been developed that have opened themselves to adding questions of race, gender, environment, and other issues to an analysis centered in (shifting) political economic conditions. Class-based movements, both revolutionary and labor-reformist, have always been stronger in Europe than in the US and so has Marxist theory as a tool for understanding social movements but important Marxist movements and theories have also evolved in the US. Marxist approaches have been and remain influential ways of understanding the role of political economy and class differences as key forces in many historical and current social movements, and they continue to challenge approaches that are limited by their inability to imagine serious alternatives to consumer capitalist social structures.

Movement Cultures

The shared values, styles, behaviors, language, traditions, symbols, and/or other forms of group definition by which a social movement marks itself as unique. A movement-specific ideology or set of beliefs is perhaps the most conscious marker of a movement culture, but much of a movement culture may be unspoken, invisible, such as a sense of connection based on shared past experiences. Tangible markers of a movement culture might include: a special way of talking (a shared slang, or movement-specific slogans); rituals or ritualized behaviors (singing in a circle, a special kind of handshake); a uniform or stylized clothing (ethnicity-specific clothing, overalls to mark sympathy with poor farmers); a symbol (a black panther, the Aztec eagle of the farmworkers flag); a movement-identified form of artistic expression (black freedom songs, Chicano murals); movement folklore (stories of past victories or defeats, jokes about an opponent's follies); identification with tradition (a hero of the past, a history of previous struggles, revival of a suppressed or forgotten ethnic custom). A variety of other terms have been suggested to name the phenomena of a movement developing a special pattern of connection, including: *movement communities, oppositional subcultures, cultures of solidarity, cultural havens.* All these have in common the sense that movements create special patterns of interaction and expression that distinguish them from the wider, surrounding culture. Movements clearly differ in the degree to which they develop a specific culture, and no movement is ever fully isolated from or free from the influences of the larger culture(s) of which it is a part. For an attempt to categorize and characterize differing degrees or intensities of movement culture, see John Lofland, "Charting Degrees of Movement Culture: Tasks of the Cultural Cartographer," in Johnston and Klandermans, eds. *Social Movements and Culture* (1995).

New Social Movement Theory

New Social Movement Theory developed initially in Europe to help explain a host of new movements that emerged in the 1960s and 1970s that did not seem to fit a model of Marxian class conflict that had been the predominant model in much European social movement theory. The "newness" of the putatively new social movements is said to consist of such things as a greater emphasis on group or collective identity, values and lifestyles rather than or in addition to developed ideologies, and a tendency to emerge more from middle than working class constituencies. The Green Party in Germany with its emphasis on environmental and peace issues, feminism, and alternative non-consumerist lifestyles is often portrayed as the umbrella group representing a synthesis of new social movements aimed at a broad, general social liberation. Some new social movement theorists emphasize a change in the economic structure of the First World from an industrial, heavy manufacturing based "Fordist" (after Henry Ford's assembly line) to a "post-industrial," "postmodern" or "post-Fordist" economy centered more around the service sector (i.e. fast food restaurants) and computer-based information industries as a structural force shaping the new movements. See Mayer and Roth, "New Social Movements and the Transformation into a Post-Fordist Society," in Darnovsky, et al. eds. *Cultural Politics and Social Movements* (1995)

Organizing vs. Mobilizing

A distinction developed by Civil Rights activist Ella Baker and elaborated by scholar-activist Charles Payne, *"I've Got the Light of Freedom"* (1995), mobilizing refers to the process by which inspirational leaders or other persuaders can get large numbers of people to join a movement or engage in a particular movement action, while organizing refers to a more sustained process whereby people come to deeply understand a movement's goals and empower themselves to continued action on behalf of those goals.

Political Process Model

The form of social movement analysis that stresses the ways in which the wider political system, especially the federal government in the US, opens up and closes down opportunities for organizing resistance. An example of the opening up would be the positive Supreme Court decision against segregation in *Brown v. Board of Education*, while an example of closing down would be the infiltration and repression of Black, Red, and Brown Power groups in the late 1960s and early 1970s by the FBI and other state agencies. The most influential example of this approach is Doug McAdam, *Political Process and the Development of Black Insurgency, 1930-1970* (1982). PPM is closely connected to Resource Mobilization Theory (see below) but looks more broadly at the political context in which movements mobilize their resources.

Resource Mobilization Theory

This school of social movement analysis, developed from the 1960s onward, has been and remains the dominant approach among sociologists, though it has increasingly been challenged in recent years. RM theory stresses the ways in which movements are shaped by and work within limits set by the resources (especially economic, political and communications resources) available to the group and the organizational skills of movement leaders in utilizing those resources. It is especially interested in direct, measurable impacts of movements on political issues, and less interested in the expressive, ideological, identity-shaping and consciousness-raising dimensions of movements. More recently, the attention of scholars in this school has been turning slowly toward some of these more cultural questions. An important pioneering work in this latter vein is Aldon Morris, *Origins of the Civil Rights Movement* (1984), which stresses African American church language and church music as cultural resources drawn upon by the early civil rights movement.

Ritual

In the context of thinking about social movements, a ritual can be defined as a structured event designed to create, enhance, and/or express the belief system and/or emotional tone of a movement culture.

Bibliography

Alex Callinicos, *An Anti-Capitalist Manifesto.* London: Polity, 2003.

Amatoritsero, *The Black Consciousness Movement in South African Literature,* (Godwin) Ede

Anthony Giddens. 1985. *The Nation-State and Violence.* Cambridge, England: Polity Press.

Armand L. Mauss. 1975. Social Problems of Social Movements. Philadelphia: Lippincott.

Charles Tilly, *Social Movements, 1768–2004*, Boulder, CO, Paradigm Publishers, 2004.

Charlotte Ryan and William W. Gamson, The Art of Reframing Political Debates. *Contexts.* 2006; 5(1):13-18.

David F. Aberle 1966. *The Peyote Religion among the Navaho.* Chicago: Aldine.

David Snow, Sarah A. Soule and Hanspeter Kriesi, ed. *Blackwell Companion to Social Movements,* Blackwell, 2004.

David Solnit, *Globalize Liberation: How to Uproot the System and Build a Better World'.' San Francisco: City Lights, 2003.*

Denton E. Morrison. 1978. "Some Notes toward Theory on Relative Deprivation, Social Movements, and Social Change." In Louis E. Genevie, ed., *Collective Behavior and Social Movements.* Itasca, Ill.: Peacock. pp. 202–209.

Diani, Mario, and Doug McAdam. Social movements and networks. Oxford University Press, 2003.

Donatella della Porta, *The Global Justice Movement: Cross-national And Transnational Perspectives.* New York: Paradigm, 2006.

Donna Maurer. 2002. *Vegetarianism: Movement or Moment?* Philadelphia: Temple University Press.

Doug Killam. *The Companion to African Literatures.* Indiana University Press (2001) (Section titled *Apartheid*), p. 29-47.

Feuer, Alan (March 17, 2009). "They've Seen the Future and Dislike the Present". *The New York Times.* http://www.nytimes.com/2009/03/17/nyregion/17zeitgeist.html?_r=1.

Gail M. Gerhart, Black Power in South Africa: The Evolution of an Ideology (1979).

Gelder, Melinda, *Meeting the Enemy, Becoming a Friend.* Boulder: Bauu Press, 2006.

George M. Fredrickson, White Supremacy: A Comparative Study of American and South African History (1981).

Graeme Chesters, & Ian Welsh. *Complexity and Social Movements: Multitudes at the Edge of Chaos* Routledge 2006.

Greg Palast interviewing Joseph Steiglitz, "IMF's Four steps to Damnation" The Observer (London), 29 April 2001: http://www.jubileeresearch.org/analysis/articles/IMF_Four_steps_Damnation.htm

Hadden, J. Tarrow, S., *Spillover or Spillout? The Global Justice Movement in the United States after 9/11*, Mobilization, 2007, VOL 12; NUMB 4, pages 359-376, online

Herbert G. Blumer 1969. "Collective Behavior." In Alfred McClung Lee, ed., Principles of Sociology. Third Edition. New York: Barnes and Noble Books, pp. 65–121.

Horwitz, Claudia and Maceo Vega-Frey, Jesse, "Spiritual Activism & Liberation Spirituality," http://www.stonecircles.org, May 2006.

Jacque Fresco "City Systems", Cybernetic Government *The Venus Project*

Jai Sen, Peter Waterman, *World Social Forum - Challenging Empires.* Black Rose 2008

James Alfred Aho. 1990. *Politics of Righteousness: Idaho Christian Patriotism*. Washington: University of Washington Press.

John Brewer, *After Soweto: An Unfinished Journey*. Oxford: Clarendon Press, (1986) ch. 4

John Walton, David Seddon, Free Markets & Food Riots. Blackwell 1994

Kwasi Wiredu, William E. Abraham, Abiola Irele, Ifeanyi A. Menkiti. (eds.) *Companion to African Philosophy*. Blackwell Publishing (2003) p. 213.

Mark Chaves. 1997. *Ordaining Women: Culture and Conflict in Religious Organizations*. Cambridge: Harvard University Press.

Mary Amanda Axford. *Mary of Many Colors: Book Review: Biko, by Donald Woods* Accessed on November 22, 2009.

Michael Lobban. *White Man's Justice: South African Political Trials in the Black Consciousness Era*. New York: Oxford University Press (1996)

Nigel Gibson. *Black Consciousness 1977-1987; The Dialectics of Liberation in South Africa* Accessed on December 1, 2005.

Smelser, Neil J. 1962. *Theory of Collective Behavior*. New York: Free Press.

Tom Mertes, "A Movement of Movements", New York: Verso, 2004.

William Kornhauser. 1959. *The Politics of Mass Society*. New York: Free Press.

Williams, angel Kyodo; Gass, Robert; Horwitz, Claudia; Vega-Frey, Jesse; Maina, Ng'ethe; Haines, Staci K.; Movement Strategy Center (2010). *Framing Deep Change: Essays on Transformative Social Change*. Third Way Press. p. 4.

Index